Do Our Pets Go to HEAVEN?

by Terry James, Thomas Horn & Contributors

DEFENDER
CRANE, MO

D0124694

Do Our Pets Go to Heaven?
Defender
Crane, Missouri 65633
©2013 by Terry James

All rights reserved. Published 2013.
Printed in the United States of America.

ISBN: 9780984825677

A CIP catalog record of this book is available from the Library
of Congress.

Cover illustration and design by Daniel Wright:
www.createdwright.com

Unless otherwise indicated, all Scripture quoted is taken from the
Holy Bible, King James Version.

The "remedies" listed in this book are included as a matter of
informational interest regarding how such remedies have been suggested
over the years. We can't, however, vouch for their effectiveness. We
recommend that animals needing medical help be seen by licensed
veterinary professionals.

Dedication

To Jeanie Hedges—in fatherly love

Contents

Acknowledgments

My most sincere thanks to my dear friends Tom Horn and his family for their heartwarming contributions to *Do Our Pets Go to Heaven?* Like the James family, they hold their beloved pets close in unapologetic embrace. That great love comes across, as the reader will soon see.

My special love and thanks to Angie Peters, whose masterful editing acumen in producing this book was—as always with her involvement in any project—nothing short of indispensible.

My deep love and profound thanks to Dana Neel for her diligence and unparalleled generosity in using her marvelous research talents and contributions to help produce this volume.

My family's love and thanks to Dr. Carol Entricken (Carol Lee) for her many years of veterinary care for our beloved pets at Benton Veterinary Hospital.

To you, the reader, our warmest appreciation for choosing *Do Our Pets Go to Heaven?* to explore the deeper aspects of the love between our pets and ourselves. Our heartfelt hope is that you will be uplifted by the experience.

—Terry James

Foreword

By Joe Ardis, Dog Behaviorist

There was a time, not long ago in fact, that I wouldn't have even entertained the concept of pets in Heaven. I couldn't imagine that the Creator of all things would bother with such a trivial matter. In fact, there was a day when I avoided the majority of the animal kingdom altogether. Well, of course I owned an occasional, modest fish aquarium (its purpose in my home far more defined by the level of aesthetics it could bring to the ambiance of my living room than by the life of the fish within), but as far as the ever-faithful companion figure depicted in every nostalgic scene of the all-American dream home, I wasn't buying it.

When I looked at happy, Norman Rockwell-style paintings of young boys in overalls hugging the family dog in the grass next to their Radio Flyer wagons, my mind would wander to a scene wherein lies only a cacophony of noise-making furry things, muddy hairballs, and dripping, soggy tongues reaching their germs toward the unsuspecting humans from beyond their unbrushed teeth. When visiting the home of someone who chose willingly to coexist with these hairy "family members," my arms would involuntarily rise into the air well above wet-nose height while I continuously backed away from the animal until it could be ushered into a back room—all the while, my eyes darting about for a gallon of hand sanitizer in the case of accidental bodily contact.

I'll admit it: My discomfort with pets, primarily dogs, was not only overkill, it was often bordering on a clinical phobia as the result of my inexperience in regards to them—an inexperience I was perfectly content to hold onto for all my days.

But that was *before* a canine companion changed my life forever...

After relentless pleading over the period of several years from the three ladies in my life (my wife and two little girls), I could no longer ignore their requests (a convincing harmony of "please Honey," "please Daddy," and one "pwease Dai-dai" from my toddler); therefore, I caved in, allowing my soft heart to pave the way for the fifth member of our family. His name was "Tank" (a mastiff/boxer mix, because why not have a "tongue-on-legs" be useful as a guardian as well as companion, right?).

Oh sure, the first day was beautiful, sentimental, and endearing—the ultimate scene to trump any Rockwell painting, indeed: proud parents looking over the shoulders of their two pajama-donned, messy-haired, bright-eyed beauties on Christmas morning as they tore the colored paper from the box and held high the wiggling prize from within. I even caught myself thinking once or twice that the puppy was rather cute. *Yeah...Maybe I really could do this. Maybe I had it in me after all to be a dog owner...*

How could I have known that by allowing this innocent present-opening ritual in my own home to include *him,* I was really attending the coronation ceremony of the new king? By nightfall, it was revealed to me who really was master over whom, as I found I'd been demoted—reduced to naught but the dog-food vending machine: a slave in service to the seemingly eternal wants, whims, and requirements of the *new* master of the house. He was hungry; he was needy; he was clingy; he chewed on stuff; he barked; he required a trainload of attention and management; he pulled against the leash at three o'clock in the morning when he should have been going potty anywhere *but* that walkway!

Oh, the responsibility.

I honestly wondered at times if there would ever be normalcy in our home again; I wondered if we would be better off without him; I wondered if the tasks of puppy rearing would ever come to an end; I wondered the things a lot of people wonder when first committing to a family pet. And then, the day he issued a possessive warning growl toward my little girl over his bone, I wondered if he would ever turn on my wife or my daughters when I wasn't around.

That day presented me with a difficult choice. In the past, I would have been tempted to re-home this dog solely based on the enormous inconveniences to our lifestyle he presented, but I had gone into the arrangement this time with determination to see him be the American dream dog for our home. After I observed his interaction with my daughter, however, my newfound determination was waning. I sat and stewed over the conundrum with confusion and doubt. Here I was, having finally done the unthinkable, opening my home to a pet with hair, a nose, and a tongue. For the sake of the family, I had embraced the duties that accompanied puppyhood, tackled all obstacles full steam ahead, and learned to grit my teeth until the reassuring, hand-to-fur contact of an animal was becoming gradually more tolerable to me. I was invested. I had even learned to...*care* about him.

But despite any progress or growth on my end in these areas, my lacking in knowledge of how to handle dog behavioral problems was suddenly glaringly apparent. It didn't work like it did in those lame Disney movies. You don't just bring home a dog, pat him on the head, toss a Frisbee, and crank out a productive and devoted family guardian who knows the difference between protecting his family from danger and protecting his bone from the family. The truth hit me like a freight train: I was going to have to get rid of the potential danger in my home, or learn to correct it—fast!

In a panic, I shared my woes with Eileen, a friend from church who runs a local dog rescue mission and pet grooming shop. (Thank you, Eileen! It all started with you...) She quickly provided my wife and me with the contact information for an acquaintance of hers who came with her highest recommendation. Within days, my first session with Daren, a dog trainer and certified pet technician, took place, and within hours of that, I had taken my first step toward true enlightenment. Daren was filled with passion and enthusiasm for the care, treatment, and rehabilitation of animals, paralleled only by his passion and enthusiasm to share said knowledge.

I learned so many things so fast—tips and tricks the likes of which were far displaced from the average, failing methods I had casually observed from other pet owners over the years. I learned that bursting into a room with your arms flailing around and voice at excited volumes when the dog is getting into something only serves to confuse a dog and invite him into your escalated chaos. I learned that shouting out the window at a barking dog in an effort to tell him to be quiet only communicates that you are happy to join him in his curious canine diatribe against the squirrel under the bush. I learned that attempting to retrieve an item from the dog's mouth via the grab-and-yank method only incites a fun game of tug-of-war. These techniques are about as effective as running around in a circle yelling, "Me too! Me too! Me too!"

Did you know that you cannot apply human psychology to an animal? Well, that's just absurd...

Needless to say, my understanding of basic dog behaviors was deficient the day I agreed to bring in our companion. Right away, it was clear that my own instincts could not be trusted, as they were greatly shaped from a lifetime of incorrect animal/human relationship concepts. It was the revealing of this dysfunction in my own nature that exposed the deepest need to abandon all that I had ever known (or thought I knew) about animals, dogs or otherwise, in trade for a *radical* change in my worldview.

Little by little, by applying the things I had learned from

Daren, small goals were met on a daily basis. We all felt it: an ongoing restoration of law and order within the home. I started recognizing a change in my dog. Yes, *my* dog. He was becoming so much more than something I merely tolerated; he was becoming a friend. Like they talk about in the movies and on TV about a dog being "man's best friend," I found myself actually enjoying his company and respecting him as his own entity with individual quirks and characteristics. In getting to know Tank, I started to truly love him as I observed the traits of his protective and affectionate personality with my family.

By opening my heart to something dramatically new and harnessing each opportunity to learn all that God would teach me in uncharted territory, I began to see God's design, and His real intention for people coexisting with animals. My stress and anxiety in relation to animals and mankind's bond with them was a result of my own weak, human nature and my unwillingness to venture out of the realm of what was familiar and secure. The more I welcomed the lessons in front of me, the more those lessons began to bleed into other areas of my life until my perspectives on many things around me had been given a complete overhaul.

However, unexpectedly, as I became closer to my clever and ever-growing tail-wagger, a profound truth halted me in my tracks.

I didn't change Tank. He changed me.

I suddenly realized that none of this was ever about my skills in training Tank. God was training me, and using Tank to do it. My enlightenment not only resulted in the heartwarming story of a narrow-minded animal-phobic reformed, it has made me a better dad, a better communicator, and a less prejudiced person in relation to subjects I may have made a snap judgment about before (such as whether a dog would be with his family in Heaven). Of course, I have reclaimed my rightful place as master of the house; we sleep through the night; Tank knows where to potty and doesn't pull against the leash; and he now knows his place when given a bone. And yes, as a family, we are now living within a healthy and pleasant balance at home, which now consists of a father, a mother, two little girls, a well-behaved guard dog, and a baby on the way.

Left here, this would be, on its own, a wonderful ending; would it not?

Yet, by learning how to communicate with one of God's amazing creations, and in the way *He* designed, our home has received a heavenly blessing that goes deeper than a well-behaved canine, and I can't help but believe that when we all get to Heaven, we will be the happy Norman Rockwell painting, dog and all.

Norman Rockwell often worked in his studio alongside a napping dog, and he kept hundreds of photos and clippings of dogs on file for reference, as he placed canines in key positions in many of his illustrations for the *Saturday Evening Post* and advertisements. In *How I Make a Picture* (1949), he cautioned other artists to depict four-legged creatures in a manner "just as carefully and understandingly as you paint the people."[1]

chapter one

Pets in Heaven
What Does the Bible Say?

By Thomas Horn

I cannot recount the number of times when, as a pastor of more than two decades and as a public and media personality since, I have been approached by an adult or child—eyes filled with questions—who wanted to ask me very sincerely if I believed their pets would go to Heaven. I often noted the apprehension on their faces, as if they feared this man who typically speaks out on "more important issues" like social or world events would find their questions trivial, especially in light of increasing human challenges facing people around the world.

Of course, most of these dear people were unaware of how often this question has come up for me and other Bible expositors. In fact, it seems to be one of the biggest secrets in Christianity: that our Western mindset has made it difficult to discuss what people in other countries as well as theologians down through time believed to be an important and theological question.

Most are also usually unaware that the Bible itself has some important things to say about the issue, and that many celebrated theologians and philosophers—past and present—concluded a long time ago based on these Scriptures that our pets most likely *will* be in Heaven.

Why is this believed?

One major argument has to do with God redeeming what He, Himself, made in the first place and called very "good." For instance, in Genesis, chapter 1, God creates "every living creature that moveth…and every winged fowl after his kind…and every thing that creepeth upon the earth after his kind: and God saw that it was *good*"(emphasis added; see Genesis 1:21–25). The Hebrew word translated "good" in this text is *towb* and means the creatures were exactly what God wanted them to be; they pleased Him. But if in the Garden, as a result of the temptation and fall of man, God *forever* lost what He created, the devil won part of the battle that day by stripping God of His aspiration. This suggests that God can never again have what He, Himself, desired in the first place—that Satan somehow permanently undid the Creator's pleasure. This is considered foolish reasoning by some doctors of theology and contradictory to other aspects of the New Testament regarding redemption or deliverance of "**all creation** [which] is waiting eagerly for that future day when God will reveal who his children really are. Against its will, all creation was subjected to God's curse. **But with eager hope, the creation looks forward to the day when it will join God's children in**

2

glorious freedom from death and decay" (emphasis added; Romans 8:19–22, New Living Translation).

The popular Christian writer and speaker Randy Alcorn is among those who believe the redemption of creation described above and in other books of the Bible such as Revelation (chapter 21) and Isaiah (chapter 65) will include pets. He writes:

Eden was perfect. But without animals Eden wouldn't be Eden. The New Earth is the new Eden—Paradise regained, with the curse of the first Adam reversed, transformed into the blessing of the last Adam (Jesus) (Rom. 5:14–15). Would God take away from us in Heaven what he gave, for delight and companionship and help, to Adam and Eve in Eden? Would he revoke his decision to put animals with people, under their care? Since he'll fashion the New Earth with renewed people, wouldn't we expect him also to include renewed animals?[2]

Alcorn's approach is shared by others who believe our pets will be in Heaven simply because we love them and God promises to give us the desires of our hearts (Psalms 37:4). For instance, in her book *Holiness in Hidden Places*, Joni Eareckson Tada says of "Scrappy," her deceased pet schnauzer:

If God brings our pets back to life, it wouldn't surprise me. It would be just like Him. It would be totally in keeping with His generous character. ... Exorbitant. Excessive. Extravagant in grace after grace. Of all the dazzling discoveries and ecstatic pleasures heaven will hold for us, the potential of seeing Scrappy would be pure whimsy— utterly, joyfully, surprisingly superfluous.... Heaven is going to be a place that will refract and reflect in as many ways as possible the goodness and joy of our great God, who delights in lavishing love on His children.[3]

Billy Graham holds similar views, and when he was once asked by a little girl whose dog had died that week whether her pet would be in Heaven, Graham replied, "If it would make you any happier, then yes, he will be."[4] Author Peter Kreeft goes even further, adding: "Why not? How irrational is the prejudice that would allow plants (green fields and flowers) but not animals in heaven?"[5]

While we believe such sentiments have merit, we also recognize that God, Himself, loves animals! He fancies their beauty and, as Pastor W. A. Criswell recognizes, "God has shown a penchant for varieties of life forms, and it would be difficult to imagine that this would not be perpetuated in the heavenlies."[6] Indeed, we find that God values His living artistry so much that He even made some of the angelic beings to reflect the animals' faces (see Revelation 4:6–8; Ezekiel 10:14). In addition to their artistic value, God loves the company of these creatures to the point that not even a tiny sparrow falls to the ground that He doesn't account for (Matthew 10:29). Another amazing example of God's concern for animals comes from the story of Jonah, in which it appears that the people of Nineveh were spared destruction because God wanted to have mercy on their children *and animals* (see Jonah 4:11)! Of course, to the delight of my wife, Nita, God is an equestrian and has already filled Heaven with lots and lots of horses (Revelation 6:2–8; 19:11; 2 Kings 6:17). His Son, Jesus, will even return someday on one such horse (Revelation 19:11–14).

It is further written in the Bible that:

- ✪ God holds the lives of animals in His hands (Job 12:10).
- ✪ He, Himself, feeds them (Psalms 104:21–30; Matthew 6:26).
- ✪ They were created for His enjoyment (Revelation 4:11).
- ✪ God never forgets about them (Matthew 10:29; Luke 12:6).
- ✪ People who mistreat their pets are judged by Him as "cruel" (Proverbs 12:10).
- ✪ Those who treat their pets kindly are called "righteous" (Proverbs 12:10).

Based on the following Scriptures, we also learn how the coming millennial reign of Christ will see animals restored to their pre-fallen conditions, and little children will be leading them about:

· ·

Horses are mentioned more than 150 times in the Bible, with the first reference found in Genesis 47:17 and the final reference in Revelation 19:21.

5

The wolf also shall dwell with the lamb, and the leopard shall lie down with the kid; and the calf and the young lion and the fatling together; and a little child shall lead them. And the cow and the bear shall feed; their young ones shall lie down together: and the lion shall eat straw like the ox. And the sucking child shall play on the hole of the asp, and the weaned child shall put his hand on the cockatrice' den. They shall not hurt nor destroy in all my holy mountain: for the earth shall be full of the knowledge of the LORD, as the waters cover the sea. (Isaiah 11:6–9)

A Question of Soul, Covenant, or Both?

Another biblical fact many pet lovers may be unaware of is that animals were created with "souls" related to what the Old Testament Hebrew text calls *nephesh*. While mankind alone was created in God's own image, and the eternal *spirit (pneuma)* of man is unique among creation, all "living beings" have "the breath of life" in them (Genesis 1:20, 24, 30; 2:7; 6:17; 7:15, 22). In the New Testament, the Greek word for this is *psyche*, which is interpreted as "mind" or "soul" and is also connected to animals in such places as Revelation 8:9. Besides these texts implying that animals can reason, feel love, and experience pain and compassion, some part of their identity may also live on into eternity. This fact was understood in antiquity and, as Randy Alcorn also documents, it wasn't until the so-called Age of Enlightenment during the seventeenth and eighteenth centuries that the concept of animals having souls began to be questioned,[7] a notion that slowly migrated into theology through secular reason, which preferred human individualism over religious tradition. Alcorn finds himself in good company among many famous Christians who likewise reject the Enlightenment position on pets. Billy Graham, C. S. Lewis, Mark Hitchcock, Dr. David Reagan, and hundreds of other clergy and theologians agree that the chances are very good our pets will be in Heaven.

But is this question of pets in Heaven a matter of "soul" alone, or something deeper…as in covenant?

In the same way that people will be in Heaven (or not) depending on their covenant relationship with God (which in the New Testament is defined as an ongoing relationship with God through Jesus Christ, our Mediator, whose atonement for our sins was made through the shedding of His blood at the cross—"this cup that is poured out for you is the new covenant in my blood" [Luke 22:20]), the question of whether pets go to Heaven may depend, some believe, on their "covenant" relationship with man! In other words, just as we are made a part of the family of God as a result of accepting the grace extended to us through Jesus Christ, pet animals may be brought back into a pre-Fall covenant by coming under and accepting human dominion as it was first intended. No longer "wild" and outside man's control, they become part of a Christian family, and are saved as a result. In this way, some animals as "pets" may be in Heaven while most other animals will not, similar to how some humans will be in Heaven while others will not, all depending on restored covenant.

The Bible provides examples of God's covenants being

extended to animals under man's dominion. Note that Genesis 9:8–17 reads:

And God spake unto Noah, and to his sons with him, saying, And I, behold, I establish my covenant with you, and with your seed after you; **And with every living creature that is with you, of the fowl, of the cattle, and of every beast of the earth with you; from all that go out of the ark, to every beast of the earth.** And I will establish my covenant with you, neither shall all flesh be cut off any more by the waters of a flood; neither shall there any more be a flood to destroy the earth.

And God said, This is the token of the covenant which I make between me and you **and every living creature** that is with you, for perpetual generations: I do set my bow in the cloud, and it shall be for a token of a covenant between me and the earth. And it shall come to pass, when I bring a cloud over the earth, that the bow shall be seen in the cloud: And I will remember my covenant, which is between me and you **and every living creature of all flesh**; and the waters shall no more become a flood to destroy all flesh. And the bow shall be in the cloud; and I will look upon it, that I may remember the everlasting covenant between God **and every living creature of all flesh** that is upon the earth. And God said unto Noah, This is the token of the covenant, which I have established between me and all flesh that is upon the earth. (emphasis added)

Also note that God promises a similar future covenant concerning men and animals in Hosea 2:18, saying: "And in that day will I make a covenant for them with the beasts of the field and with the fowls of heaven, and with the creeping things of the ground: and I will break the bow and the sword and the battle out of the earth, and will make them to lie down safely."

Thus, the theory that pet animals—as creatures brought under dominion and made part of a family—will be in Heaven seems reasonable, as reflected in the original Garden of Eden, where man was subject to God while the animals were subject to man. It is likewise interesting that, when God created a covenant with a person, He usually marked that agreement by naming or renaming the individual. He did this with Abraham, Sarah, Paul, and so on. But note that God had Adam name all the animals that were to be under his dominion in the same way we name our pets today and make them part of a family unit. Author C. S. Lewis used this line of reasoning to conclude that animals made into pets and thus renewed in covenant from wild to domestic would likely be in Heaven, sanctified as an extended part of mankind's covenanted family. Lewis penned his thoughts on this belief more than once, including metaphorically in his book, *The Great Divorce*. In a scene in which a woman is arriving in Heaven with a large number of pets, a spectator begins a conversation with his angelic guide with a question:

"And how…but hullo! What are all these animals? A cat—two cats—dozens of cats. And all those dogs… why, I can't count them. And the birds. And the horses."

"They are her beasts."

"Did she keep a sort of zoo? I mean, this is a bit too much."

"Every beast and bird that came near her had its place in her love. In her they became themselves. And now the abundance of life she has in Christ from the Father flows over into them."

I looked at my teacher in amazement.

"Yes," he said. "It is like when you throw a stone into a pool, and the concentric waves spread out further and further. Who knows where it will end? Redeemed humanity is still young, it has hardly come to its full strength. But already there is joy enough in the little finger of a great saint such as yonder lady to waken all the dead things of the universe into life."[8]

In a more serious and intellectual treatment on human and animal suffering, including the possibility that pets will be in Heaven, Lewis wrote in the conclusion of his 1940 book, *The Problem of Pain*, what I personally consider one of the best arguments in this regard I've ever read. I have therefore included a large excerpt from his masterful argument as follows:

Finally, there is the question of justice. We have seen reason to believe that not all animals suffer as we think they do: but some, at least, look as if they had selves, and what shall be done for these innocents? And we have seen that it is possible to believe that animal pain is not

God's handiwork but begun by Satan's malice and perpetuated by man's desertion of his post: still, if God has not caused it, He has permitted it, and, once again, what shall be done for these innocents? I have been warned not even to raise the question of animal immortality, lest I find myself "in company with all the old maids." I have no objection to the company. I do not think either virginity or old age contemptible, and some of the shrewdest minds I have met inhabited the bodies of old maids. Nor am I greatly moved by jocular enquiries such as "Where will you put all the mosquitoes?"—a question to be answered on its own level by pointing out that, if the worst came to the worst, a heaven for mosquitoes and a hell for men could very conveniently be combined. The complete silence of Scripture and Christian tradition on animal immortality is a more serious objection; but it would be fatal only if Christian revelation showed any signs of being intended as a *systeme de la nature* answering all questions. But it is nothing of the sort: the curtain has been rent at one point, and at one point only, to reveal our immediate practical necessities and not to satisfy our intellectual curiosity. If animals were, in fact, immortal, it is unlikely, from what we discern of God's method in the revelation, that He would have revealed this truth. Even our own immortality is a doctrine that comes late in the history of Judaism. The argument from silence is therefore very weak.

The real difficulty about supposing most animals

to be immortal is that immortality has almost no meaning for a creature which is not "conscious" in the sense explained above. If the life of a newt is merely a succession of sensations, what should we mean by saying that God may recall to life the newt that died today? It would not recognise itself as the same newt; the pleasant sensations of any other newt that lived after its death would be just as much, or just as little, a recompense for its earthly sufferings (if any) as those of its resurrected—I was going to say "self," but the whole point is that the newt probably has no self. The thing we have to try to say, on this hypothesis, will not even be said. There is, therefore, I take it, no question of immortality for creatures that are merely sentient. Nor do justice and mercy demand that there should be, for such creatures have no painful experience. Their nervous system delivers all the letters A, P, N, I, but since they cannot read they never build it up into the word PAIN. And all animals may be in that condition.

If, nevertheless, the strong conviction which we have of a real, though doubtless rudimentary, selfhood in the higher animals, and specially in those we tame, is not an illusion, their destiny demands a somewhat deeper consideration. The error we must avoid is that of considering them in themselves. Man is to be understood only in his relation to God. The beasts are to be understood only in their relation to man and, through man, to God. Let us here guard against one of those untransmuted lumps of atheistical thought which often survive in the minds of modern believers. Atheists naturally regard the co-existence of man and the other animals as a mere contingent result of interacting biological facts; and the taming of an animal by a man as a purely arbitrary interference of one species with another. The "real" or "natural" animal to them is the wild one, and the tame animal is an artificial or unnatural thing. But a Christian must not think so. Man was appointed by God to have dominion over the beasts, and everything a man does to an animal is either a lawful exercise, or a sacrilegious abuse, of an authority by divine right. The tame animal is therefore, in the deepest sense, the only "natural" animal—the only one we see occupying the place it was made to occupy, and it is on the tame animal that we must base all our doctrine of beasts. Now it will be seen that, in so far as the tame animal has a real self or personality, it owes this almost entirely to its master. If a good sheepdog seems "almost human" that is because a good shepherd has made it so. I have already noted the mysterious force of the word "in." I do not take all the senses of it in the New Testament to be identical, so that man is in Christ and Christ in God and the Holy Spirit in the Church and also in the individual believer in exactly the same sense. They may be senses that rhyme or correspond rather than a single sense. I am now going to suggest—though with great readiness to be set right by real theologians—that there may be a sense, corresponding, though not identical, with these, in which those beasts that attain a real self are in their masters. That is to say, you must not think of a beast by itself, and call that a personality and then inquire whether God will raise and bless that. You must take the whole context in which the beast acquires its selfhood— namely "The goodman-and-the-goodwife-ruling-their children-and-their-beasts-in-the-good—homestead." That whole context may be regarded as a "body" in the Pauline (or a closely sub-Pauline) sense; and how much of that "body" may be raised along with the goodman and the goodwife, who can predict? So much, presumably, as is necessary not only for the glory of God and the beatitude of the human pair, but for that particular glory and that particular beatitude which is eternally coloured by that particular terrestrial experience. And in this way it seems to me possible that certain animals may have an immortality, not in themselves, but in the immortality of their masters. And the difficulty about personal identity in a creature barely personal disappears when the creature is thus kept in its proper context. If you ask, concerning an animal thus raised as a member of the whole Body of the homestead, where its personal identity resides, I answer "Where its identity always did reside even in the earthly life—in its relation to the Body and, specially, to the master who is the head of that Body." In other words, the man will know his dog: the dog will know its master and, in knowing him, will *be* itself. To ask that it should, in any other way, know itself, is probably to ask for what has no meaning. Animals aren't like that, and don't want to be.

My picture of the good sheepdog in the good homestead does not, of course, cover wild animals nor (a matter even more urgent) ill treated domestic animals. But it is intended only as an illustration drawn from one privileged instance—which is, also, on my view the only normal and unperverted instance of the general principles to be observed in framing a theory of animal resurrection.[9]

Whether C. S. Lewis' argument in favor of pets making it into Heaven is as convincing to others as it was for me the first time I read it, there is one final point I would like to add: Animals are included with men as those who are commanded to praise the Lord! This was true in the Old Testament in places such as Psalms 148:10–13, where we read:

Beasts, and all cattle; creeping things, and flying fowl: Kings of the earth, and all people; princes, and all judges of the earth: Both young men, and maidens; old men, and children: Let them praise the name of the Lord: for his name alone is excellent; his glory is above the earth and heaven.

And this amazing fact—that animals praise the Lord—will also be true in the future, as they are seen offering praise unto the Lamb of God extending into eternity in Revelation 5:13:

And every creature which is in heaven, and on the earth, and under the earth, and such as are in the sea, and all that are in them, heard I saying, Blessing, and honour, and glory, and power, be unto him that sitteth upon the throne, and unto the Lamb for ever and ever.

chapter Two

The Animals
God's Gift to Man

By Terry James

You've just lost your friend. He, you now know, meant far more to you than you ever realized while he was alive. No longer will your friend bounce cheerily up to you with his favorite toy in his mouth, or rub lovingly against your leg, seeking no more or less from you than a few words of baby talk and a scratch behind the ear. Your old companion of many years, perhaps a dog you chose from a litter more than a decade ago, has passed away from the ravages of age. Maybe the bright-eyed cat who was your constant shadow when you were doing things of interest has just been hit by a car in the street not far from your front door. Their hearts have been stopped by death, the ultimate fate of every living thing—but your heart beats on sadly within a void that, it seems, can never be filled.

Regardless of where you try to turn your thoughts, no matter how you try to busy yourself, the memories both recent and distant flood your mind and make the emptiness more painful. You remember the enthusiastic greeting that met you when you returned home. You go over in your mind the silly ways your friend reacted to your attentions. Your throat constricts with emotion, and the tears come—whether the remembrances are of the last time you had to use harsh words and corrective measures, or of the sparkling, dancing eyes and happy grins of playful joy the last time the two of you engaged in a mutually favorite game. The thoughts just keep coming.

There comes a time when your friend's absence becomes less agonizing, the many thoughts and words of consolation having mercifully helped you get past the worst of it. It is a time the injury caused by the awful loss is no longer an open wound, but tender scar tissue that can be abrased open by finding a toy behind the sofa or in a bush along the corner of the fence. At such a moment, you might glance toward that other corner of the yard, where the now down-sifting mound of raw earth disrupts the grass. The thought of your beloved friend lying lifeless beneath the dirt there brings a wince and more tears. You've thought about it before, but now you are able to better govern your emotions, enabling you to focus your thoughts for deeper consideration.

What about animals?

Do they have spirits?

Is there a Heaven for our dear little animal friends?

Your friend, you remember, would look at you on many occasions when your eyes met, and you knew there was intelligence; there was emotion, feeling, and genuine love in that instant of two-way communication. Many of your human friends, probably most of them—especially those who have no pets—sympathize with your loss. Nonetheless, you sense they consider your deep love for your pet-friend to be perhaps just a bit silly.

"I know it was just like a member of your family," your human friend might say, uncomprehending. He or she cannot understand that the one you've lost is not an "it," nor "like" a member of the family. Your friend *was* a member of your family. The feelings, the communications, the understanding that passed between you and your pet-friend had a spiritual quality that transcended mere human-animal contact. You say to yourself in the quietness of that empty place in your heart: "They can't just die and that's the end of them."

This writing admittedly springs from such an empty spot, the author having recently lost as close a friend as one could have. At such a time it is easy, through upset emotional senses,

If Adam—the first human charged with the task of naming an animal— was still around today, he might be interested to know that "Max" for males and "Molly" for females hold the top spots in the list of most popular dog names, with "Max" and "Chloe" heading the list of most popular cat names.[10]

to philosophize—perhaps a better word in this case would be *theologize*—that I will see my wonderful bulldog friend in a future where time is meaningless and death is unknown (read about Buckley in chapter 9). But the thought that Buckley and I *can* be together again is not, I think, based purely upon blind emotion or sheer wistfulness, an issue my friend Tom Horn has authoritatively addressed in our first chapter. This is not to imply that I believe our animal-friends have spirits or souls in the same sense that human beings have souls. I believe, however, like Tom and many others, that the pets we love so much, with whom we've shared such deep feelings of devotion in two-way spiritual communication, can achieve life after death. The animals, you see, were *created for us*.

> And the LORD God said, It is not good that the man should be alone; I will make him an helpmeet for him. And out of the ground the LORD God formed every beast of the field, and every fowl of the air; and brought them unto Adam to see what he would call them: and whatsoever Adam called every living creature, that was the name thereof. And Adam gave names to all cattle and to the fowl of the air, and to every beast of the field. (Genesis 2:18–20a)

> And God said, Let us make man in our image, after our likeness; and let them have dominion over the fish of the sea, and over the fowl of the air, and over the cattle, and over all the earth, and over every creeping thing that

creepeth upon the earth. So God created man in his own image, in the image of God created he him; male and female created he them. And God blessed them, and God said unto them, "Be fruitful, and multiply, and replenish the earth, and subdue it; and have dominion over the fish of the sea, and over the fowl of the air, and over every living thing that moveth upon the earth." (Genesis 1:26–28)

It is so very important to understand that the animal world was created for us...that our pets exist for the pleasure our love for them gives us.

chapter three

Our Funny-Looking Children

By Terry James

"*Candid Camera*"-*type* television shows and numerous TV commercials often illustrate similarities between owners and their pets. Amusing similarities they can be! A man with a long, sagging face and mournful, bloodshot eyes sits sleepily alongside his equally drowsy basset. A tall, sleek woman with pretty, sharp facial features and tawny, flowing hair holds a leash at the end of which strains a magnificent Afghan hound. A corpulent woman with wide, curious eyes set within her equally expansive but nonetheless lovely face, clutches a fat, furry Persian cat whose expression tells you "we were destined to be together." If such episodes of *Candid Camera* or such TV commercials can be considered an art form, then certainly real life does more than imitate art in the matter of people and their pets. To those of us who truly adore them, they aren't pets at all. They're simply our funny-looking children.

Those who observe us treating our pets like humans seldom understand this attitude we have of regarding our animal friends as family members. As a matter of fact, even those we know who treat their own pets in exactly that way often consider our behavior odd, or perhaps even ridiculous. Although I have intensely loved every one of my own pets, I must admit I sometimes view as just a bit excessive the profuse affection my relatives, friends, and acquaintances sometimes lavish upon their animal friends. But isn't that true of relationships in general? Our young children's noisy playfulness is marvelously funny and endearing to us and to Grandma and Grandpa, but such behavior might be the most abrasive of irritants to an outsider.

We have all, at one time or the other, visited others in their homes and, once in the door, had to shake a feisty poodle or Pomeranian off our leg while trying to converse civilly with our hosts. In those moments of aggravation at the yapping and snarling of pets eagerly seeking our attention or expressing displeasure at our presence, it is not so easy to either believe in or desire the possibility of life after death for these little troublemakers.

But these are, like our own pets, our hosts' family members. They are their "children" in furry, funny-looking clothing. When death takes these pets we love, we are diminished greatly. The grief is profound. In our valley of despair, it doesn't matter what others think of the intense love we have for our departed friend.

It *is* a much-appreciated human friend, however, who takes the time express, in whatever way he or she chooses, that nothing is silly or ridiculous about grieving the loss of a loved friend—be that friend human or animal.

Nothing in our relationship with our pet friends brings more delight than watching them do the funny things they do. The more humanlike their mannerisms, the more endearing they become. On the flip side, remembering those charming mannerisms becomes bittersweet recollection of these delightful friends and companions. It hurts all the more when they pass away.

We often fail to recognize that it is we who impart to them the humanlike characteristics we love so much. Their individuality absorbs a part of us, their human mommies or daddies, not unlike the way in which our own children are molded by the home environment we provide for them. This is probably why we don't recognize our own pets' irritating ways when company calls…why we feel visitors should love our pets as much as we do. Our furry friends are like a part of us, and when they are rebuffed by the people around us, we, too, feel rebuffed: "If you don't like my pet, you wouldn't like my children either; therefore, you must not like me." Spoken or unspoken, consciously recognized or not, this, to me, seems to be the psychology within human-pet relationships, at least in America,

> To give your dog or cat relief from the irritation of flea bites, try adding a teaspoon of vinegar to each quart of your pet's drinking water.

where such relationships enjoy the luxury of a higher degree of development than in many other societies. (See chapter 17 for a snapshot of Americans' spending on—and spoiling of—their pets.)

While I fully admit that I have been put off by pets whose human parents allow them to behave poorly, I have—perhaps hypocritically so—never spoken openly of my displeasure of the behavior of other people's pets while I've been in their homes. There have been occasions when people visiting my home who don't share my affection for my pets have not been quite so... *tactful*.

Since my animal friends, like my children, have never been less than well-behaved—for they have been, you see, under my good influence—I naturally feel visitors to my home have no grounds on which to find fault with my furry children any more than they would to find fault with my human children. Such criticism directly assaults me as a parent.

Knowing that you consider the above comments in the lightheartedness with which they were made, I now turn toward the more serious side of our purpose in this book. The reason we wrote the book and the reason you are reading it is to look at our relationships with these marvelous little (sometimes large) companions in an eternal context.

Like our relationships with our human loved ones, interaction with our pets, we must acknowledge, has some imperfections. These "down times"—the puddles in the middle of the kitchen floor—are necessary. They give contrast and clarity—that is, substance—to the wonderful memory-images of our friends that we will carry with us until it is our time to join them in that forever called eternity.

Hopefully, this book will help us to firm up a few conclusions about what that afterlife means for us and the pets we love. Surely we can, at the very least, stimulate thought and conjecture about the issue of life after death for the pets we love so much.

I ask you for your patient indulgence while we journey toward this goal. Our chosen vehicle for taking us to our destination is constructed of several biographies, word-picture portraits, of my own family's and another family's "funny-looking children." I look forward to the bright future day when I will have mine gathered about me again. They will, I'm certain, be full of life and vigor…and sporting those happy expressions of joy that will never end.

. . . .

References to dogs in Matthew 15:25–27 and elsewhere seem to indicate that dogs might have been kept as pets in those ancient days—perhaps even inside—as they were close enough to the eating area to eat crumbs off the floor. Interestingly, cats are not mentioned in the pages of Scripture.

L assie is perhaps the most beloved celebrity canine of all time. The silken-haired, brown-eyed beauty made her screen debut in 1943, in the movie, *Lassie Come Home*. She had her own radio show, then switched to TV in 1954, winning two Emmy awards before the show's end in 1973. Known for her loyalty, selfless devotion, heroism, and intelligence, she is one of only three dogs to have her own star on the Hollywood Walk of Fame (along with Strongheart and Rin Tin Tin).

chapter four

Butch

By Terry James

Angels are appointed to watch over pets—of this I feel certain. Butch and our wonderful time with him convinced my family and me more than a decade ago. His story is one of an odyssey rivaling those in Greek mythology, at least in our view. But Butch's story is absolutely true. Memories of our all-too-brief time with him still bring broad smiles and tears of emotion-tugging nostalgia.

Butch's odyssey began a number of years before he came to us. We really don't know how old Butch was. We figured he must have been in the neighborhood of three or four years old when finally our seven-year-old son managed to, as we still put it, "conjure him up." When you have read the story, perhaps you will agree with us that Butch's angel and our son, Nathan's, angel, must be quite good friends. The whole matter is just too strange to be otherwise.

Nathan's green eyes flashed brightly when we asked the traditionally inevitable question as Christmas approached. "What do you want for Christmas?" He didn't hesitate. "I want a bulldog." Now Nathan, at that age, loved stuffed animals of every description, so our natural inclination was to begin thinking in terms of a stuffed toy bulldog. This would be a request easy to fulfill; we thought little more about the matter, knowing that Santa would have at least one thing checked off of his list for Nathan. However, when our younger son's desire became all-consuming to the point that it was "bulldog this" and "bulldog that," we finally concluded that Nathan was talking about getting a **real** bulldog.

We had had one dog, an Airedale terrier puppy named Max ("Lord Maximillian of Yorkshire," as his name appeared on his AKC registration papers). Nathan hadn't yet been born and our other son, Terry Jr., then five years old, was, like us, a cat person. Samantha, a beautiful Manx who looked more like a small bobcat than a housecat, had been with us about one year. However, we foolishly thought that it was necessary that a boy be raised with a dog. We lived in a townhouse apartment, which anyone with any degree of sensibility should have realized is a living situation not conducive to raising a puppy who—almost overnight—turned into a huge, energetic dog. We, of course, in all our wisdom about such things, considered the apartment the perfect environment for the boy and his puppy.

We were wrong.

Max soon ate, or tried to eat, most of the apartment, including the carpet on the stairs leading to the upper rooms. Wonderful dog though he was, Max didn't deserve to be subjected to our family as situated at the time: He was better suited for a nice family more land-endowed than were we.

Max had his own angel, too. That became evident, when upon taking him to the vet for some routine maintenance, we casually threw out the comment that we would be willing to give him up for his own sake if the aforementioned "nice family" with ample land for him to rove freely could be found in the area. Of course, there was a further stipulation. This "nice family" would have to have some children young enough to keep up with Max's energy and to love him. The veterinarian who was examining Max patted him on the head, glanced at us, and said, "Don't worry. I'll be right back." About fifteen seconds later, the doctor returned with a woman following close behind. "This is my part-time assistant," he said as he introduced her.

"What a beautiful Airedale!" she exclaimed, lovingly rubbing Max's head. He licked her hand. It was an instant match.

"I told her you might give him up under the right circumstances," the veterinarian said.

"We live on a farm just a few miles from here," the woman said, still admiring Max and baby-talking to him while playfully scratching him behind his ears. She said she had children at just the right ages to give him all the roughhousing and adventure he could handle. Then she said the clincher. "We've been praying for a dog just like this. We wanted an Airedale and checked them out, but just couldn't afford one. How much do you want for him?"

I looked at Margaret and she looked at me. What else was there left to say? "He's yours," I voiced our mutual answer.

The mother who would soon take Max to his new home and his new friends was elated and effusive with gratefulness. Max seemed equally jubilant and returned her warm affection in his normal, wet-tongued fashion. The doctor told both us and Max's new owner that he would see to it that Max never lacked for free medical attention. Altogether it was a happy time, although there was a rather large empty spot in our hearts for a while. Terry Jr., who was then as he is now, quite clinical in his personality and assessment of matters, helped assure us that Max would be better off on a large farm with a family who loved him, and that he would be better off with just himself and Samantha, his beloved cat pal. I've always felt that there was one other individual involved in the whole transaction: a very pleased angel who silently and invisibly vowed that he would make up for our loss of Max at just the right time and place.

Dogs, then, had been out of the picture and out of mind, really, for all these years since Max, and now Nathan, seven years younger than his brother Terry, was devoting all his creative energies to thoughts of bulldogs. Pictures started turning up everywhere....cut out of magazines, torn from newspapers, even pointed out on television programs. The most inescapable of all the bulldog pictures were those drawn by our almost artistically talented Nate, who also attached a name to the pictures: "Butch."

"Do you think I'll get a bulldog for Christmas?" he asked at least daily. "Where will you get a bulldog?" "Have you ever seen a bulldog, a real bulldog, I mean?" "It could stay in my room, couldn't it?" "I'd name him Butch." The running commentary on a bulldog named Butch filled our ears, usually accompanied by a picture, a line-drawing of Nathan's version of a bulldog—underneath which was scrawled the name.

Apparently Nathan's strategy was working, because Margaret and I eventually began wanting a bulldog, too—even though we had never even seen one in "person." It seemed as if a bulldog was there somewhere, just beyond our grasp. I have to think that Max's angel knew that the time and place of repayment for our earlier kindness was drawing closer. He must have been working overtime to see to it that the time and the place intersected at the point Nathan's burning desire for a bulldog and Butch's great need for an adoring family met in one God-ordained moment of love at first sight.

Our many conversations about bulldogs, about the specific bulldog named Butch that Nathan wished to be a part of our family's future, naturally began to spill over even into our work lives—Margaret's, in particular. Her company was, at the time, a closely knit circle of people who were not merely coworkers but friends. Nathan's Holy Grail-like quest for Butch the bulldog had grown by now to near-legendary proportions, and Margaret would often share with her colleagues Butch's portrait as rendered by her one-track-minded son. Obviously, mothers worth their salt couldn't help but become involved in Nate's all-consuming, almost holy crusade to produce a bulldog named Butch.

Then it happened. The fantasy began taking on form and substance. One of Margaret's friends at work—Karen—told

Margaret that she had heard about a bulldog who seemed to belong to no one running free in a community not far from our home. The dog, Karen said, was often seen by her husband while he made deliveries in the area. As a matter of fact, her husband had told her, he frequently stopped his truck when he spotted the dog, who always came to him for petting and a kind word. The bulldog was running with a number of other dogs and apparently had trouble keeping up with his longer-legged pals. Karen's husband wanted to bring him home, but she was less than enthusiastic about the prospect. Thus began what is still known today in the James family as "the bulldog patrol."

The bulldog patrol began within minutes of Nathan hearing that "his" bulldog was roaming free not five miles from our house. His mother's green eyes sparked with excitement while she explained the plan for us to institute "bulldog patrol," a search that would go on for several weeks. I must admit to a great deal of enthusiasm that first afternoon we drove to the little housing addition, my eyes (before the onset of the disease that led to my blindness when I was in my mid-thirties) scanning every yard, every porch, every street. The trips to the area became less frequent with each patrol that failed to produce the dog, but Karen's deliveryman husband still told stories of the bulldog who was infatuated with the large, black delivery van; the dog continued to come to the truck each time her husband stopped to offer a pat and a kind word.

So, bulldog patrol never really ceased to be a part of our activities. Certainly Nathan's one great passion never cooled in the slightest degree while we continued to review his—by this time—more sophisticated renderings of the bulldog as described to his mother by Karen's husband. Hope yet burned within us all, until the day Karen's husband reported that the bulldog no longer seemed to be in the area where he had previously always encountered him. The other dogs were there, but "Butch" was missing—a fact that only strengthened Nathan's resolve to find him.

Time and place converged in what I will always believe was an angelically executed miracle one afternoon when Nathan's mother drove toward a small store a mile or so away from our home to get something we needed. The road she was on is a highway, really, leading from a busy thoroughfare in our town to a large plant in the business of producing aluminum byproducts. As Margaret neared the street she would turn on to in order to reach the store, she spotted an object about as long as it was wide and about as tall as it was long in the middle of the highway. One of the most compassionate animal lovers there is, she instantly recognized the bulky object as being animal, not inanimate.

"It's…it's…it's…a bulldog!" she later told me she had exclaimed to herself while trying to brake. "It was just as if he was sitting there like he was on a leash," she would later tell me.

I was working at my desk that day when sounds of a struggle just outside my office caught my attention. In a moment, the door opened, and Margaret, hugging a large animal, her arms wrapped around its chest just beneath its front legs, strained to walk with the beast a few feet farther before depositing it as gently as she could near my feet.

"Look! It's a bulldog!" she exclaimed excitedly between

attempts to regain her breath. "He was just sitting there in the middle of Alcoa Road!"

Sure enough, it was an English bulldog—tired, dirty, his ribs showing just a bit from malnourishment, but a beautiful bulldog nonetheless.

"Hello, Butch," I said.

Nathan's mother and I were flabbergasted by the way things had turned out. We discussed then, and still do to this day, the incredible set of circumstances surrounding Butch joining our family.

Not Nathan. He wasn't flabbergasted. He knew all along that we would find Butch—or that he would find us—and, though very happy to at last have Butch with him, he never gave the miraculous meeting a second thought. Like all of the children each of us at one time was, he simply accepted it as a part of the delightful world he awoke in every morning, and he lavished upon Butch all the love that was in him.

Butch responded in kind—in a bulldog sort of way (only those who have ever had a bulldog as a family member can truly understand)—allowing us to make a fuss over him and occasionally working up the energy to play a brief, though arousing, game (of his own choosing, of course). He quickly regained the weight he had lost from his meanderings. His broad, white-with-brown-spots head and neck with a dark auburn body beautifully marked with areas of white made him look as if he were wearing a World War II air corps bomber jacket. "Bomber Bob," as we nicknamed him, soon blossomed into his full potential, his broad chest and shoulders rippling with thick muscles. The one flaw, according to AKC standards, so far as we could tell, was that he had only one testicle, which was most likely the reason, we were later told by a breeder, that Butch had been turned loose to make his own way in the world. His left back leg, slightly atrophied due to having been damaged most likely in an accident, was his only other physical problem. (We had learned about Butch's limp long before we ever met him personally, from hearing the description of the dog by Karen's husband.)

Butch continued to snap to attention anytime he saw one of the dark delivery vans, the vehicle he had come to love while roaming free. Whenever he was out in the yard, he could hear the engine roar blocks away as it made its stops and starts, and he eagerly awaited the truck's arrival.

Still a traveling man, at every opportunity Butch took off in whatever direction met his fancy. So when he was outside, we had to stay with him unless he was on a leash or in the "fence that Butch built," the structure we had erected especially for him when he joined the family.

An amusing twist to this strange story is that the name of Karen's husband is Butch. I am pleased to report that Butch (the deliveryman) and Karen (who wanted nothing to do with having a bulldog) are now the proud human stepparents of a beautiful little female bulldog named Sassy.

The veterinarian said that no one knew why for sure that dogs are susceptible to developing ear polyps, but Butch soon showed evidence of tiny cauliflower-like growths inside both of his ears. We kept his ears meticulously clean like the doctor instructed, awaiting the time when the polyps had developed to the point that they could be surgically removed. The growths were affecting Butch's hearing when we finally could take him in for the treatment, which the veterinarian told us would involve burning the polyps and hopefully getting to the roots of their origination. He warned that frequently they return.

Parting with Butch was hard for all of us as we watched the vet's assistant lead him into one of the clinic's back rooms, where they would keep him overnight without food in preparation for surgery the next morning. We called as soon as we thought the surgery might be completed, and were elated to hear that Butch had come through the procedure just fine. We could come and pick him up after another day of recovery. The doctor said his ears would require constant attention for a while, but then should begin to heal nicely.

All went on schedule, the ears healing, and the affected areas responding well to the medicine and cleansing agents the doctor gave us to apply. Within a month, however, signs of regrowth appeared in the ear canal, and it was another trip to the clinic, where the veterinarian told us that, more than likely, the polyps would keep coming back no matter how many surgeries like the previous one were performed. However, there was an alternative procedure, the doctor said, a more radical procedure in which the ear canal was opened from the outside and the tissues cleaned out all along the ear canal. This procedure had a relatively high-percentage chance of getting the seed roots of the polyps. The surgery would be rather expensive, and the procedure would involve a bit more risk than the previous operation.

The doctor said that without this more involved procedure, the polyps would almost certainly return.

Our little friend with the flight jacket, sitting on the stainless steel examining table, of course, was the same as our child, as far as we were concerned. A little funnier looking than our other two, maybe; just about as stubborn, perhaps—but, nonetheless, he was one of us. We would have the surgery no matter the cost.

The assistant again led Butch to the back room of the clinic, this time without so much trepidation on our part. The recovery would take longer this time because of the more involved circumstances. We were told that we should be able to pick him up in a couple of days. Meanwhile, we were to call and check on him anytime we felt the need. I watched Butch walk through the door, tiredly, unlike his usual way when he tugged enthusiastically at the leash.

· · · · ·

There is no way to be prepared, whether the announcement is about a person you love or an animal you love. There is just no way to prepare.

"Mr. James, I've got some bad news," the head of the clinic said sadly over the phone. "We lost old Butch."

Animal shelters report that between 20 and 30 percent of the dogs they receive are purebreds.[11]

My mind darted quickly to the thought of Butch as I had last seen him walking slowly into another room at the clinic with one of the veterinarian assistants. Did Butch somehow get out the door in a back part of the building, and was he now roaming free, as he would have preferred because of his former liberty to roam about as he pleased, enjoying the canine hobo life? My thoughts snapped back to the voice at the other end of the line.

"It was his heart. He just couldn't take the strain of the anesthesia. I did everything I could think of to bring him out of it, but he just wouldn't respond to anything."

A flush of comprehension soaked my emotions. I was silent for a moment. "We don't blame you, Doctor, I know you did everything possible for him," I said, able for some reason to discern the emotion in the voice of this man who had been a veterinarian for thirty years or longer. "You told us there was always a risk..."

"I'm really sorry. Short-nosed breeds like the bulldog can have real respiratory and pulmonary problems. He might have had a congenital problem."

"I know you did all you could do," I repeated.

"Would you like for me to have them clean him up so that the family can see him?"

"Oh...no... I don't think any of us could take that," I said, a decision I later regretted.

"We can take care of him for you, if that's what you'd like us to do," the vet said with compassion in his voice.

"That would be best."

One high, dry corner, where the steel fence "that Butch built" meets now is home for the remains of three cats and a dog. Butch, however, was never brought home for burial, and I have regretted that hasty decision ever since. My thought at the time was to spare Margaret and the boys from having to deal with seeing a freshly disturbed spot in the yard, but in retrospect think I made a decision as much for myself as for them. Butch had his angel; of this I'm sure. That angel, I equally believe, knows exactly where Butch's spirit resides and will, it is very important for me to believe, have his heavenly leash in hand at just the right moment when it is needed.

The bulldog's strength, aggression, and appealing personality have made it a common mascot for sports teams and universities. Perhaps the most famous bulldog is the University of Georgia's Uga, who has (in a series of eight incarnations) appeared at almost every one of the team's football game since 1956.[12]

Sometimes bulldogs and other breeds tend to develop lesions and swelling between the toes. To reduce puffiness, soak the affected paw in a saltwater solution (1 tablespoon of sea salt in a small bucket of warm water) for a few minutes. Pat dry, then apply tincture of iodine to the area.[13]

chapter five

Samantha

By Terry James

Samantha was certainly no angel. As a matter of fact, we often referred to her as the "cat from hell"—but not because of the way she treated us, for she was a totally devoted member of the James family. She earned that designation for the somewhat less-than-gracious way she dealt with any cats who came anywhere near her territory. And the whole world, so far as she was concerned, was "her" territory. With dogs, it was another matter. Samantha liked dogs.

She was a Texas girl, brought from Tyler along with her mother, sisters, and brothers, to a rural town in southern Arkansas where my grandmother lived. Her mother was a calico named Margot, and her father, we were told, was a "traveling man," a beautiful, big, blue-gray Manx who looked like a lynx. According to the description of her father, she was his spitting image, even though four months old. She had long ears and a muscular body with a hiked-up rear end, atop which sat a tiny stub tail. Her front legs were like those of a normal cat, but her rear legs looked very much like a jackrabbit's. And as she grew, they began to look more and more like the legs of the cartoon character, Wile E. Coyote, after he had swallowed some muscle-building pills from the Acme Corporation, from which he frequently ordered devices in his never-ending quest to capture the Road Runner.

Samantha was blue-gray in color with faint calico markings. Her fur was thick, as were her extraordinarily tough claws. She looked forever more like a bobcat kitten that spring day I reached up to take her from the small tree in my grandmother's backyard.

The last cat Samantha ever truly got along with was Sheba, a kitten about her age we had gotten from a friend less than a month earlier. Sheba, gray with black stripes, met us when we returned to our apartment with Samantha a hundred miles later, quite delighted to have us home again. Sheba's overwhelming curiosity caused her to circle the cardboard box we set on the kitchen floor upon arrival. When we opened the box, our new kitten popped out, and Sheba stiffened much like she had been zapped with a shock of electricity, her fur puffing. The sight of this strange-looking beast caused Sheba to completely forget herself and leave both her dignity and bladder control on the kitchen floor. The two kittens hissed and bowed and backed warily from each other, each finally seeking and finding her own hiding place from which to consider what was going on.

In a very short time, Sheba began to take matters into her own hands (rather, paws). The country-bumpkin whatever-it-was—this strange-looking beast with no tail—obviously, in Sheba's view, needed to be taught the sophisticated ways of city feline living. Samantha was reluctant. She remained reluctant in the matter of receiving any sort of instruction till the day she died, as a matter of fact. Still, Sheba didn't give up. The slick city girl finally managed to interest the country cat in a game of hide-and-seek, and eventually the two were engaging in the rough-and-tumble play all felines of their age relish.

By the time Christmas rolled around, the two, now much larger, were the best of friends. Sheba, always the quicker wit-ted of the two, managed to disappear whenever something got broken, leaving Samantha to catch the brunt of our wrath when we found the pieces. Maybe that is what turned her against cats. Like, for example, that Christmas when Margaret and I came in one afternoon late to find the Christmas tree ornaments scat-tered about the floor, some broken, others strewn about the apartment. Samantha, still the country girl, lay stretched across the artificial branches at about the mid-tree level looking very relaxed and blinking at us. Sheba was nowhere to be found.

Margaret shooed Samantha from the tree and began clean-ing up the ornament mess. I straightened the branches as best I could before going into the bedroom to look for the other cat. I couldn't find her, so I began the daily ritual of getting undressed after a day's work, part of the routine being to place various items within a chest of drawers. I noticed one of the drawers was gapped about three inches, so I pulled it open fully and Sheba, obviously feeling a degree of guilt, was tucked neatly in the drawer and looking up at me as if to say, "I've been here all along." How she managed to close the drawer after getting in is a mystery we still talk about. Perhaps it was Sheba's angelic caretaker trying to watch out for her.

Soon we were to move six hundred miles away to another state, and would have to give up one of our kitten friends. We kept Samantha because of her unique characteristics and because she had been a "family cat" from her beginnings (it was my aunt and uncle who had brought her from Tyler, Texas. Margot, Samantha's mother, was their cat.) Our downstairs neighbor, an unmarried man in his late twenties, was delighted to adopt Sheba in to his household despite their traumatic first encounter when she scratched him in her fear and uncertainty over being removed from familiar surroundings. We knew that if he could still pick her up and baby talk to her, trying to calm her fears after such a violent encounter, Sheba had someone who would truly love and care for her.

Terry Jr., four at the time, loved Samantha from the start, and the feeling seemed totally mutual. They were seldom apart when we were at home. Their closeness remained to the end of Samantha's days on earth more than eighteen years later.

Those years brought many interesting and sometimes astounding events involving our bobcat family member—like the time she brought home an unexpected visitor from the wooded area she loved to explore not far from our house.

Samantha had been spayed the moment she went into heat. Very early in our married life, Margaret and I had had experiences with female cats in heat; it is, to put it mildly, quite an annoying thing with which to become involved. But the experience convinced me that we didn't need to endure it again. When your normally dignified, serene cats (at least during the moments they are not turned back to the playtime of their kittenhood) go into the natural though totally obnoxious throes of the feline pro-creation process, human-animal relationships, no matter how lovingly close, quickly become strained to the breaking point. Thus, my vow—"never again!"—was quickly fulfilled the first time Samantha made amorous overtures to anything and every-thing she touched or that touched her. A quick visit to the vet and a day's recuperation restored the young cat back into the Samantha we knew and loved.

Still, we all wondered what kind of mother Samantha might have been. We received at least a partial answer seven years later, when, upon my opening the front door, Samantha calmly strolled into the house with a large, furry, dark object clinched snugly between her teeth. Margaret, as she always does under these animal circumstances, quickly left the room with a shriek and the announcement to everyone within earshot that Saman-tha had a dead animal in her mouth. The cat walked to one cor-ner of the room, near a table, and very gently deposited her furry package. My older son and I examined it from a distance; it was a dark-brown, baby cottontail rabbit—bright-eyed, and appar-ently unhurt. Samantha walked a few feet away and sat down looking first at us, then back at the rabbit. It was as if she was asking us for an explanation of exactly what kind of thing this was. She made no further move toward it; she simply looked at us and then back at the rabbit, which sat there tentatively but not fearfully.

We picked the bunny up and checked it out. Its skin had not been broken in any area. It had been carried as gently as any mother cat would carry her kittens. Samantha quietly watched us handle the rabbit, showing no desire to have it returned to her. Of course, we went into a great deal of detail explaining to her that this was a baby rabbit, and that she could neither kill it nor adopt it, but that we would be happy to take care of the problem for her. So Terry returned the baby to the wooded area, hoping its mother would find it in the safe place he chose. The best I can recall, Samantha yawned, stretched lazily, and found a place to sleep.

One conclusion I draw from this encounter of the odd kind is that even baby cottontails must have angelic watchers over them. I have also concluded that Samantha did not always react to other animals as "the cat from hell."

Samantha, hellion though she sometimes seemed, had an angelic watcher, too, as was made almost supernaturally clear one late afternoon while she explored the tiny moving things that often served as her prey in our front yard. Remember, she had always detested cats of any description. Dogs were quite another matter. I had always wondered over the way in which she reacted to dogs. She would either lean up against them and use them as a rubbing post, or would simply glance at them, maybe sniff them, then treat them as if they were nonentities. Never did she hiss or react in typical cat fashion when confronted with a canine encounter.

That afternoon, while I stood several yards from her doing something or the other on the front lawn, I saw in the distance a huge black form loping toward us. A big Doberman pinscher, its teeth bared, growling viciously between half attempts to bark, ran straight for Samantha, who had been playing with bugs or grazing on grass or whatever. My first panicked thought was, "I will never get there in time to keep that dog from killing her." My next thought was, "Why doesn't she run?"

The Doberman, even larger than he had looked from that distant point where I had first spotted him, suddenly threw on the brakes, coming to a sliding halt not three yards from Samantha. She had calmly turned from her grazing and now walked the several feet to where the perplexed dog stood, ears erect and tongue hanging between its huge fangs in a panting sweat from his sudden burst of energy a few moments earlier. The cat went to the Doberman, put her nose up against his nose, and sniffed once or twice...then turned and resumed her full attention on what she had been doing before. The Doberman had by this time reverted to his puppyhood, his tongue hanging from his cheek in the silliest of ways, his ears pricked forward. He bounced all around her playfully, his tailless rear up in the air while his front half scooted along the ground, first toward her, then side to side. It was an unbelievable sight: A twelve-pound cat totally ignoring a dog that must have weighed at least a hundred pounds. Somehow, Samantha knew that there was no need to worry. (Perhaps she sensed her angel lingered nearby.)

> If your cat or dog develops itchy ears, lubricate the inflamed area with aloe vera or vitamin E oil.

Samantha, through those eighteen and a half years of life with our family, never so much as sneezed because of illness, as far as I can remember. She ruled the animal family within our household, which included at one time or the other Max the Airedale and Butch the bulldog; Simone, an adult Siamese who was full grown when she came to us; Felix, the smartest cat in the whole world; our much-loved Cato, Katie, and Cala; and, of course, my wonderful pal and constant companion, Buckley. Of those beloved pets, only Cala, a beautiful white Siamese mix with bright blue eyes and personality to match, lived during the reign of Her Royal Highness, Queen Samantha. She empirically tolerated all but Simone, who gave her very wide berth. While during her most vigorous years she could easily cower even the neighborhood's biggest tomcat bullies (of all her many fights, her only injury was a slight notch in the tip of one ear), she enjoyed the well-deserved respect of all the animals in the vicinity with the exception of any new neighbor-pets who had not yet crossed her path—and, of course, young Felix.

To Felix, the elder though still tough Samantha was nothing more or less than a wonderful old toy to pretend attack at every opportunity. Although she could have done him great bodily injury with very little effort if she had wanted to use those still-lethal claws and teeth, I never saw her do more than bat him across the room once or twice. I'm almost certain that I more often than not saw a sparkle of matronly maternal amusement in the old cat from hell's yellow eyes whenever Felix, a male kitten with Persian-like features who was about the same color as herself, fearlessly made his assaults. I am convinced, too, that more than once I saw in her reactions to him her royal approval.

Both bulldogs—Butch and, later, Buckley—during their respective times under Queen Samantha's regime, were granted full privileges of access to her. Butch, already full-grown when he came to us, for a time had trouble figuring out this tough, strange-looking family member named Samantha. He would sit on one hip with one leg tucked beneath him and the other stretched long, and glance at her sheepishly out of the corner of one eye while she approached to sniff him, then walk beneath his always-wet jowls, taking full advantage of his rubbing-post qualities. He would shuffle, somewhat disconcerted, trying to get a quick sniff of her while she went on her way. The canine pals he used to run with—what would they think of this? A cat that would not break and run?

She raised Buckley (more later about him), and rarely ever became irritable with his puppyhood shenanigans. When, ultimately, Samantha had to be taken to the vet so that she no longer would have to endure the sufferings of her old, diseased body, her bulldog friend looked for her for days and moped pitifully. So did I.

· · · · ·

Samantha reached to touch me that last day of her life. She always pulled at my clothing or my bare skin with those bob-cat-like claws when she wanted my attention. She was skin and bones, and no doubt in pain stemming from cancer or some other disease, but still she wanted a moment of closeness that, of course, I sadly gave her. We had waited too long, no doubt, to make the inevitable decision that had to be made. I told her I loved her and gently rubbed her in the ways she had always enjoyed, then I walked from our bedroom, leaving her on top of the chest of drawers where she often perched during her last years. This tough, old cat had been a family member for almost two decades, and now came the time to perform the final, heart-breaking act of love.

Someone else in the family had to do it. They always do in this matter of dealing with putting a pet to sleep. I haven't the courage.

While the others drove Samantha to the clinic where the vet would give her relief from her terrible suffering, my thoughts replayed over the many years. That stub-tailed little cat in that tree at my grandmother's home; the heavier, dumb, country-bumpkin

. . . .

The cat's meow: Cats may lack the facial expressiveness of dogs, but they more than make up for it with the many varied vocalizations, ranging from a friendly, all-purpose "hello" to a "chirp" or "trill" a mother cat uses to tell her kittens to follow her. Ultimately, the housecat's royal cousin, the lion, takes the prize for most effective communication skills; however, the lion's roar can be heard from up to five miles away.

cat sprawled across the branches of that artificial Christmas tree; the incident with the baby cottontail; the confrontation with the Doberman; the notched ear; the way she always commanded attention when she desired it—the affectionate remembrances of those many years brought a bittersweet smile that masked a heart heavy with the emotion of losing my feline daughter. Somewhere in that dark corner of gloom, however, there flashed the briefest illumination of belief that we could be together again someday.

chapter six

Felix

By Terry James

Felix is a fellow who has always taken matters into his own hands (rather, paws). He has done so from the very beginning when, as a tiny kitten, he demanded to be a part of the James family. Surely his angelic watcher must have taken an amused delight in that mouthy little cat who, obviously displeased with his circumstances, screeched his way into our hearts that hot summer afternoon while Margaret and I walked and jogged the local high school track. I've always wondered if Felix's angel perhaps gave his diminutive furry ward a slight nudge, urging him beneath the high steel fence that day.

Because we already had two cats at home, neither of whom liked the other nor any other cat, I opposed the idea of plucking this loud-mouthed kitten from its track-side residence. I was certain that if we circled the track enough times, the little cat would go back to its mama, and Margaret would see the wisdom in leaving it there. I knew the battle was lost when the kitten grew more vocal while following us as closely as he could and Margaret reached to pick him up.

"He's so skinny," she said pitifully. "He hasn't been eating."

Cats have for a great many years now lived in the area just outside that fence. A very nice lady with a heart full of compassion for animals still feeds them daily and their numbers have grown considerably. The majority of the cats who live there are of the black variety and want nothing to do with humans—except for their faithful human foster mother, who shows up every afternoon with their food. Felix, on the other hand, was from the beginning a people person who waited on no one and nothing; rather, he took command in every situation. We knew instantly that this extroverted little cat was no relation to the black-cat colony and presumed that most likely someone wanting to get rid of him had reasoned in his own insensitive way that by dropping him off with this colony of cats he at least would not starve to death.

But he was hungry. The other cats hadn't hurt him in any way, but it was obvious that neither had they invited him to partake of "grandma human's" daily dole of food. Having analyzed

. . . .

Cats have thirty-two muscles in each ear, and can move them in different directions at the same time.

all of these things, I gave in to Felix and his new "mother," and we added to our household one very big mouth to feed.

Felix is a delight and absolutely the most intelligent feline I have ever known. He is a superb hunter, although his mother counts this as a distinct negative rather than a positive trait. I've watched Felix take a number of kittens under his attentive tutelage, all of whom adored him and tried to emulate his every move. When we've lost some of the kittens to accidents and others to illness, Felix, though always dignified and noble in his manner, has mourned each loss in his distinct way, even sitting serenely by each gravesite while Terry Jr. carried out the burial chores.

To give human attributes and characteristics to our animals is perhaps a foolish exercise. But observing Felix and considering the special way in which he came to us makes it impossible for me to believe that this wonderful cat will simply turn to dust when his time comes to never be a part of my experience again. Any personality, be it human or animal, who contributes such joy to our odyssey through this earthly life, surely must do so not only in the physical realm but on the spiritual level also. If that is stretching belief to the outer limits of reality, I'm nonetheless satisfied with and comforted by the thought.

> If your cat has a wound abscess that is draining, rinse the area thoroughly with the following solution (wear protective gloves): 1 pint of water, ½ teaspoon salt, and ½ teaspoon echinacea/goldenseal tincture.

One of the cartoon industry's most iconic characters, Felix the Cat was the "first image to be broadcast over the television airwaves…[because] the engineers at RCA Research Labs…used a rotating Felix doll as their test model in their very first transmission on NBC."[14]

chapter seven

Cato, Katie, and Cala

By Terry James

Cato entered our lives in an unspectacular way, but soon proved to be a kitten if not with a spectacular personality, certainly one unique from any feline I had ever known. His coat was white with just a hint of beige; his ears looked as if they had been dipped in lavender gray ink, with similar markings spread at just the right spots on his tail, legs, and face. His sky-blue eyes betrayed his absolute devotion to having a good time. That was his happy-go-lucky personality. Cato was the only cat I have ever known who could, from the time he was old enough to climb up in my lap, relax to the point that if I didn't restrain him from falling, he would literally pour into the chair or floor as if he had been spilled from a glass. When you picked him up, he was totally limp. He delighted in forcing us to contain his body, that is, to keep it from slithering downward to the next level. He would then stiffen his body and, with play viciousness, attack without warning. Thus, he quickly earned the name Cato (because he was of the Oriental variety and because he constantly employed clever attack strategies, we named him after Chief Inspector Jacques Clouseau's Chinese valet in the *Pink Panther* movies.)

Samantha, of course, was totally miffed at Cato's arrival and would speak to no one for days because we had not consulted her majesty before bringing him into her kingdom. Simone, Cato's fellow Oriental, hissed and spat and stared at him as if she wished him dead (they obviously spoke different dialects of Chinese). Buckley, by now the stodgy British resident who spent a great deal of his hours during the day sleeping, sniffed the kitten and was quite tolerant when the little one would pepper his face with play attacks or bite an ear. Buckley would snort as bulldogs do and would show displeasure when Cato got into his ultimate attack mode only by shuffling his huge front feet, panting a little heavier, and following the little cat a little more closely with his stately brown eyes. Felix instantly took Cato in hand and began trying to teach him all he knew about the quickest way to make a kill and other vital things. As Felix has done with all his cats, he would hold Cato down with one big paw, nuzzle the little cat's chin upward, and then gently put his big jaws around Cato's throat. This was to demonstrate a "practice kill," a thing that Cato quickly picked up and began to try to do to Buckley. However, he could manage little more than a mouthful of dewlap skin hanging in folds beneath Buckley's always-wet jowls.

Cato's attempts to "practice kill" Samantha on several occasions ended with his being batted across the room or being pummeled for several seconds in her fury. Still, she showed her merciful side, allowing him to live to attack another day.

Felix—by this time, "Uncle Felix" (we gave him the honorary title because of his extraordinary patience with and attendance to his adopted nephew, Cato)—strolled casually one day into the house, a small kitten the same shade of gray as himself following closely behind. She looked very much like Felix had looked the day he had called to us at the high school track in his loudest, most grating voice. She was quite thin, but apparently a little older than Felix was when we found him, because she moved more steadily on her feet than he did when he joined the family. Uncle Felix had found a niece, we believe, because he felt that this little orphan cat needed a loving home, and, of course, a lively playmate for the always-attacking Cato would free up some of his time, particularly his naptime whenever he came in from his many adventures with the wild things he had to deal with in the wooded creek area behind our home.

We had difficulty finding a name for this little cat for some reason. Margaret finally settled on the name Katie. She was not a pretty cat, but rather plain, with no outstanding features, physically or personality-wise. She was just a plain gray little cat, much like Uncle Felix was when we first got him. But she was much quieter.

Cato, of course, attacked at first opportunity, but gently and carefully, because he wasn't sure just how powerful an adversary he might be facing. Katie, for a day or so, withdrew into whatever corner she could, hissing at everyone in the animal family except, of course, Felix, whom she loved. They all love Felix.

Her first glimpse of Buckley brought the same reaction that it brings to most cats who had not yet met him: She bowed her back and looked very much like the stereotypical Halloween cat frightened by some passing witch. Buckley, as usual, sniffed her once or twice, then went over to one corner to sit and observe her for a while. It wouldn't be long before Katie—like Felix, Cato, and Samantha—would be loving Buckley and rubbing up against him, walking beneath his mug, and making sure that the top of her body got totally soaked by his wet face from the top of her head to the end of her tail. Simone, on the other hand, sometimes rubbed against Buckley, but she seemed to prefer a dry pass rather than a wet one.

Katie stayed neither plain nor without personality. She grew to be a slick-haired beauty who, when sitting erect in her tail-wrapped position, could easily pass for a magnificent Egyptian statuette. But that beauty was to develop later; during her time with Cato, she served as a wonderful sparring partner with growing grace and athletic ability, which the beautiful though somewhat clumsy Cato didn't possess. They spent many happy hours playing in paper sacks, in cardboard boxes, and many other makeshift hiding places. Uncle Felix would sometimes join them, but only briefly before either being called outside to his creek-patrol duties or else falling asleep in the most comfortable place of his choice. We were a whole, happy family—both human and animal.

• • • • •

There is a time and a season for everything under Heaven, and our Samantha's time came. She withdrew more and more from the animal members of the family as her age-caused illness sapped her energy. She grew listless and meowed loudly for reasons we couldn't understand, probably because of pain she didn't understand. She could no longer hold down food, although she never stopped eating; her weight dropped dramatically, and her eyes bulged as her body shrank. It was time to let her spirit return to the One who gave it, and so we sadly agreed to make her return quick and painless.

The others didn't miss her too much because of their youth and fast-paced activities. It was a different story with Buckley. He missed her very much, and looked for her for days. He seemed to mope in a depression that not even his little admirers Cato and Katie could lighten. Eventually, though, the hurt of losing Samantha lessened with the healing that time brings and with the knowledge—at least among Samantha's human family members—that she had been very sick and in pain, but now she was at rest.

Old age and its suffering, with the diseases and disabilities it inevitably brings, makes death sometimes seem a bit less the villain. But when life is snatched from the young—no matter how it happens—death seems all the more cruel. So it was that when Cato was struck by a car late one afternoon, living no more than a few minutes afterward, our family's peace was shattered once again as when Butch had left us several years before. Margaret took it particularly hard, perhaps because Cato had come to our home through one of her friends, or perhaps more correctly, because Cato had had a special love for his "mommy" and invariably gave her a special paws-on greeting whenever she returned home from her various errands. Our little white, blue-eyed almost-Siamese cat of less than one year in age had always been at her side while she went about her kitchen duties or when she sat on the floor to knead bread dough, which he often tried to steal chunks of.

Uncle Felix, too, showed signs of grieving, having watched Cato die and then, as he always does, stood by the grave into which his much-loved nephew was gently lowered. Katie, although missing her playmate for a time, finally turned her playful affections to Uncle Felix and Buckley, neither of whom seemed able to have a heart for the little cat's rambunctious games.

Katie soon grew to be the sleek Egyptian beauty described earlier, with personality to match. Her bluish-tinged gray coat glistened while she moved about the house in silence and aloofness. Her only vocal response came when she voiced her displeasure over being touched when she didn't want to be, usually a low, whining growl, the sort that in other cats would be a forewarning of a more vicious response. This we came to know as simply Katie's way of responding to everything—whether she liked it or whether she didn't. She would growl if we pleased her, and she would growl if we displeased her.

It was always a great honor when beautiful Katie condescended to spend a few moments in our laps. We were expected to pay her the proper amount of attention, which meant not too much physical contact while she lay there. Any more than a couple of strokes down her long, perfectly proportioned back, and we would be given the growl of irritation. If, when she was in a certain mood, we stopped the stroking before we should, we received a growl of displeasure for being so insensitive to her needs. We loved her very much in a growing sort of way.

It seems that we scarcely had time to really begin loving her for the truly wonderful friend she was when she was taken from us by the same cruel specter that had taken our Cato a few months earlier. Katie was struck by a car in the street in front of our home, not far from the spot where her playmate/stepbrother had been hit. Ironically, both were killed in the same place, on the same day of the week (Friday), at almost the same hour (5 p.m.).

Cato's death brought us his niece, Cala, a beautiful white cat with the Siamese markings very similar to those of her uncle. Cala's big, blue eyes and slightly clumsy agility somewhat relieved the terrible hurt and emptiness we felt with Cato's passing. Cala's personality was much like Cato's while she moved about the house, sometimes involving herself with Margaret's activities of bread-making or other interesting things being done by the human family members. She, of course, was totally taken with Uncle Felix the first time she laid eyes on him. Felix, as always, gave her as much of his time and attention as he could afford, which was less than usual by now because he had a number of feline friends with whom to patrol the creek area, thus was out of the house more. Within a couple of days of coming home to live (Margaret's friend had personally taken her to the farm where Cato's sister and her first litter of kittens were living in a barn), the little cat was using the bulldog, as did all of Buckley's cats, for a rubbing post. She seemed not at all concerned when his huge mouth would clamp his cavernous wet jaws over her little body and employ a gentle play bite or two. Buckley seemed to know that this little cat somehow was linked to Cato, and I think I sensed in him the same need for consolation after having lost Cato as did the rest of us.

It didn't take long for this little white ball of energy to melt the serene Katie's aloofness. The two of them were soon engaged in play as vigorous as when Katie and Cato stalked and chased and rustled about the house. Although Katie could easily out-smart and outmaneuver little Cala, she always seemed to see that her young friend got her share of the victories. When Uncle Felix finally managed to arrange his busy schedule so that he could properly teach "practice kill" to Cala, his adopted niece almost immediately tried the technique on Buckley, as had her Uncle Cato. Only now, Buckley applied his own version of "kill-the-cat" by engulfing the little white body in his gigantic jaws. The only danger this presented, of course, was the possibility of her drowning from the water that constantly dripped from his mouth because of the many drinks his hot-natured bulldog body required from the big water bowl near which he liked to hang out.

Cala could bellow most mournfully when she really wanted something badly. Sometimes, we couldn't interpret exactly what she felt she needed so desperately, but on those occasions, Margaret in particular would scramble to do whatever she could to satisfy Cala's unhappiness. Cala rarely made noises at other times, except for an occasional grunt when we picked her up, because she had grown so plump from her many trips to the feeding area just off the kitchen. But when she did make her voice heard, we had no doubt that, at least in her mind, all was not well. Usually, however, the loud cries involved no more than a closed door that she felt needed opening so that she could go about her routine exploration, or they sometimes meant she couldn't find Katie or Felix. Or maybe Simone would pay her no attention. Soon the little cat—who grew quickly into a beautiful, plump cat—would forget her unhappiness, and we would find her in a favorite window perch watching the outside activity, or laid up in a very un-catlike position on her side or back, her head propped up against the snoring Buckley, both of them sound asleep.

Thus, it was all the more heart-rending when Cala's mournful cries were for real when our beloved Katie was killed that Friday afternoon near where Cato had been struck by a car. I thought Margaret was just a bit paranoid about her reluctance to let the younger cats out of the house. She was not. I realize now that her motherly instinct about the dangers in this fast-paced world that surrounds us with streets of asphalt and drivers who are inattentive to the dangers they present to our children and our pets was correct. Katie, a very intelligent cat, had become disoriented that afternoon, and when a car going three times the speed limit roared down the street, she dashed into its path rather than back toward the front door. She was killed instantly.

Cala was inconsolable, searching for Katie in every room, her wails making our own grief even harder to bear. She seemed to seek solace and an explanation from everyone. Her constant companion since she had arrived at our home, one with whom she had shared even the uncertainty of the trip to the animal clinic for their spaying operation, and the recuperative period that followed once they had returned home, could not be found. That we could not explain to her why Katie was no longer with us made the parting even more painful.

Time, love, and Cala's short memory span soon soothed her terrible loneliness. Not so for Margaret.

She had not grieved so openly or so deeply for Katie as she had for Cato a few months earlier, but the empty spot in Margaret's life that was once filled by the beautiful, uniquely-tempered Katie seemed to grow larger rather than smaller with the passing of time. We began to search the newspapers and ask friends about kittens who might be old enough to join our family. I was always certain that there would never be a shortage of cats, given their reproductive proclivities. This did not prove to be the case for that period of weeks we searched for a kitten—not to replace Katie, because that was impossible—but to make her absence from our lives just a bit more tolerable.

Margaret and I talk constantly about Katie and the things she did—we always go over all of our departed pets' endearing traits time and time again until the healing process has done its work—all the while scanning our newspapers and enlisting our friends and acquaintances in the search for news of kittens up for adoption. We made a trip to an animal control center, but were informed that the cat we had been told about had already been taken. The other cats were full grown, thus would almost certainly create problems within our animal family should we bring one of them home. It is highly unlikely that a full-grown cat, never having met the likes of Buckley, could feel at ease in its new environment. If one could reason with animals, all would be well. Buckley's gentleness despite his powerful, vicious appearance, could be explained. If, as was sometimes the case, a human was terrified just by looking at him and hearing his many bulldog snorts and mouth smacking sounds, a grown cat, no doubt accustomed to being chased by every dog it had come across, would never relax long enough to get to know what a wonderfully soft touch our Buckley was. No, adopting a full-grown cat was definitely not in the best interest of either the cat or our family at this time.

Then Margaret spotted it. A tiny ad in the classified section of our local daily newspaper. "Three kittens to give away. Two gray one black." Moments later, Margaret was on the phone. Her countenance—and, I must admit, mine, too—no doubt, had brightened considerably. Margaret explained carefully to Cala that she was going to look at some kittens, asking, "Wouldn't a little black kitten be wonderful?" I don't remember Cala's response, but I'm certain that her wide blue eyes must have sparkled with some interest, because whether she ever fully understood or not,

. . . .

Felix's "practice kill" maneuver is no inconsequential quirk of personality; it's a deeply instinctive behavior of all felines, whose keen hunting skills are enhanced by a unique stride: When they walk, their hind paws follow the fore paws in almost exactly the same place, upping the stealth factor and keeping tracks to a minimum.

she always seemed to listen with a curious expression whenever we spoke to her with an inflection of excitement in our voices.

"Wouldn't a little black cat be really wonderful?!" Margaret then put the question to me with delight in her voice. I thought to myself that even a baby baboon would be "really wonderful" if it could pull the family, both human members and animal members, out of the pit of depression into which Katie's death had thrown us.

"Sure, go have a look at it," I said to Margaret, who I don't think really heard me because of her haste to get into the car with Nathan to make the trip of several blocks from our house. They returned in less than thirty minutes, each cradling a furry ball and grinning happily.

"The black cat was taken already, but these two weren't, so…"

We lost one and gained two. That's how it usually is when it comes to cats in our family. I really didn't mind, though, and in a few minutes was running my finger up and down the sofa, getting one of them or the other to attack my finger or a piece of twine, or a pencil, or whatever was handy. Cala, usually quite relaxed as her Uncle Cato had always been, was now in a stiff, erect, Katie-like pose, her ears pricked up and her eyes wide while watching the new arrivals' every movement. When Felix came in, he gave the little sisters a quick look and went to the kitchen for a snack. He had seen many kittens come to the James household—as a matter of fact, you will remember, he had brought one into the family himself, so it seemed that he considered it nothing to get either excited about or to be alarmed by.

Simone, on the other hand, was quite miffed, as usual. Her perfect Siamese disposition, her blue-green, slightly crossed eyes flashing disdain, remained intact. She wanted nothing to do whatsoever with the two intruders. She feels the same way to this day about them.

Buckley came from his bedroom (our bedroom) when he heard Margaret lavishing baby talk upon the two little ones, his broad bulldog head cocked slightly and his brown eyes wider than usual with curiosity. Always a cat fancier, Buckley bulled right over to the sofa and thrust his big face first into one of the kitten's sides and then into the side of the other, then he sniffed, then he snorted. (We always believed him to be a bit allergic to cats.) This caused both of the kittens to bow their backs and spit at him in a typically frightened feline manner. This, of course, didn't dissuade Buckley, who put his big paws on the sofa's edge to get a much better smell, causing both kittens to back into one corner and finally accept Margaret's consoling protection. Thus satisfied that it was nothing more than a couple of new cats, the bulldog returned to his room to complete an already long nap. Little did he or we realize his future role in the upbringing of the kittens, one in particular.

Have you ever had a kitten who would not use the box? No matter what you tried, no matter how many scoldings, cajolings, or disciplines you administered, the cat would not use the litter box. So it was with one of these little gray sisters. As even the most avid cat lover will attest, a cat who cannot or will not use the litter box can quickly turn one's home into something that smells more like the cat house did the last time you visited the zoo. This particular little gray sister was quickly dubbed the "bad cat." The other one, naturally, because she was the perfect example of tidiness in litter box usage, was termed "the good cat." They later became simply Good Cat and Bad Cat, and now we simply refer to them as GeeCee and BeaCee.

Cala almost immediately began mothering these little darlings. Not much more than a kitten herself, she, at the same time, engaged them in rousing games so that we were sometimes awakened in the middle of the night with loud banging and other noises as they went about their play period. Felix took occasional swipes at them, but they were as yet too young for him to teach "practice kills" and the really important stuff, like how to stalk a squirrel or a blue jay. So he contented himself for the most part in observing them from his lofty perches.

Their new foster mother, Cala, tried everything she could think of to make Bad Cat toe the line when it came to litter-box etiquette. She met with no better success than did we, but seemed to manage a much better level of toleration and patience with BeaCee's toilet indiscretions than did her human parents.

We consistently put the little cat in the box, but she was repulsed by that vile act and would jump out, shake her feet, and disgustedly trudge off. On some occasions, Cala somehow managed to herd BeaCee into the litter box and then would stand guard, trying to keep her from getting out until she had accomplished the purposes Cala intended for her to accomplish. Cala sometimes would demonstrate for the little cat. All was for naught; she wanted no part of the litter box. It was Felix who finally, many months later, somehow sparked BeaCee's interest in using the litter box. We aren't really certain how he did it; we just know it worked, and that's more than enough for us. We did see the two of them walk into the litter box area on one occasion, Felix then demonstrated, and when he left to observe, she got in the box and did as neat a job as he did. This, of course, confirmed my long-held contention that Felix is perhaps the most intelligent cat, at least in the continental United States.

Cala was a superb substitute mother for GeeCee and BeaCee. She spent many hours with them in play and in teaching them the practice of good feline hygiene. We've watched the kittens take turns, Cala holding them down and licking their heads and bodies until their fur was wet. And as we watched, each little cat in her turn would clean each other and attempt to clean Cala, who was always tolerant of their practice hygiene, no matter how involved she was with a nap or something or other. Felix, too, joined in the cleaning sessions on occasion—all in all they were perhaps the tidiest cat family in town.

If your cat or dog suffers from arthritis, give a gentle massage starting from the center of the body and work outward, keeping in mind that sometimes feet are too sensitive for massage. Provide a soft bed made of egg-crate foam or other materials and cover with washable fabric.

℞

BeaCee and GeeCee often slept with Cala—rather, on Cala—in positions as if they could nurse her. Or they would gather around Buckley while he took one of his many naps, in emulation of Cala, using his big body for both a pillow and a blanket. Buckley's tolerance for the many cats around him reached a new and hilarious level when Good Cat took up with him in a very special way (about which, more later).

Family life is turned upside down and inside out when a house fire strikes. Everything changes within a matter of seconds. So it was with us that Saturday evening when a bedroom suddenly burst into flames due to an electrical fire.

Cala was the eternal center of the James animal family through those intervening weeks when we human members were required to stay elsewhere during the reconstruction of our home. The little white cat gave comfort to all the others during that early spring with its sometimes uncomfortably cold, dark nights and the dampness that seemed to blanket the empty shell of the house devoid of light and warmth and the constant human love and companionship they had always known. She saw them through it all, rallying them around the big, warm bulldog. We often found the kittens, when we would check on our pet family at night, piled up around Buckley, or on him, with Cala protectively hovering around. She saw them through it all, and then, in a tragic instant of violence when the hour was very dark and late, she was gone from us.

It seemed so senseless, the loss of this wonderful little surrogate mother of our animal family. Our sons found her not far from where Cato and Katie had been killed, and so another small grave, its digging and Cala's burial attended by a serene but distressed Felix, graces that high, dry plot where the fence that Butch built meets in the corner of our yard.

Those big, marvelous blue eyes often come to mind when I think of Buckley or of the two kittens now more than half grown, or when I rub Uncle Felix behind his ears. The Creator was in those blue eyes and in the love that little cat shared so openly with all of us. He is in all things good. My trust is in Him, that He loves even more deeply than we are capable of loving. And how we did love little Cala.

Remember Morris the Cat of the 9 Lives cat food commercials in the seventies? The large, finicky Tom cat—an orange tabby—went on to enjoy a lucrative career in movies alongside stars including Elliott Gould (*The Long Goodbye*) and Burt Reynolds (*Shamus*). Three different cats have played Morris since he was "discovered" at a Chicago animal shelter in 1968, with the current cat reportedly living with his handler in Los Angeles.[15]

chapter eight

Life after Death (Theirs and Ours)

By Terry James

My good friend Tom Horn did a superb job in chapter 1 of making the case for our belief that our pets will be in Heaven. After having related the many stories of my family's pets to this point, I think it good here to—I hope—reinforce Tom's reassuring words of comfort by adding my own on the subject.

Is there life after death for the pets we love? The title of this book encompasses an almost-consuming wish/desire/need that resides in the broken hearts of those who have just lost their much-loved animal family members. Death is a thing that somehow seems far off to us until it strikes close to our hearts, disrupting every part of our lives, even taking from us restful sleep, those quiet corners of solitude to which we can sometimes escape the harsher reality of life. We can think of nothing but the one whose absence we feel so terribly, and the bone-chilling finality of that separation. We have been separated from our friend before, but only by time and distance, not by the black forever that is eternity. No longer will we see the shining, adoring eyes or feel the tender, loving, playful nips and pawings, nor will we ever again be able to hold our small friend in a cuddling, nuzzling grip of love or our large animal-friend in a hugging, joyful embrace. "Dead" is an unbearable word in our time of grief.

Nothing can take away or lessen the sorrow during those first few hours, days, or perhaps weeks and months; that is a truth akin to physical law. Our totally grief-immersed emotions can be healed to one degree or another only by the ointment of ever-moving time. To truly lay hold of the belief that you can see your beloved friend again—that you **will** see him or her again—becomes more than merely a comforting thought to convey you through your grieving process; it becomes a strengthening glue that helps hold together faith that life is infinitely more than what our physical senses can confirm…that there is life after death—REAL life—for us and for the pets we love.

"Prove it!" the skeptics will say. Of course, tangible proof, proof that one can see, feel, and touch, is not available for presentation. (However, my near-death experience, as documented in my book, *HeavenVision*, as well as the accounts of many others, come as close to providing tangible proof as one can get.) The many studies on life after death and the first-hand experiences of those who have, for a time, been allowed a glimpse into eternity, all point to one conclusion: It boils down to a matter of faith.

This is not to say that we who are living can simply visualize, or wish, a thing and make it come to pass. That is not faith; it is occultism. The faith referred to here is the belief and acceptance that the Creator of all things has a great, eternal purpose for all He creates. That purpose is good because He is the perfect good, thus is deserving of our absolute trust.

Trusting Him means, among other things, that we absolutely believe that He would not create us and the world about us and then forget about us—not if He is truly good. Thus, our belief, our faith, must include acceptance with certainty that God also would not lead us without His good and perfect guidance by which to navigate life's sometimes troubling, sometimes dangerous, course. The most comforting aspect of our trust in Him comes from the belief that He has not left us to flounder, but has, in His perfect goodness, given to us His Holy Word by which to conduct our lives. He feels our sorrow, our pains, our hurts. How do we know this? Because His Word tells us so.

"But thou, O Lord, art a God full of compassion, and gracious, and long-suffering, and plenteous in mercy and truth" (Psalms 86:15). God, then, knows our most secret sufferings, including the terrible pain of emptiness and loneliness we feel when death takes a beloved pet. Doesn't it therefore stand to reason that He would address, through His divine Word, this, one of life's most agonizing hurts?

Keeping in mind that God's words to us must be considered

in their totality and not simply on a single word, verse, or passage, let's look at what He has to say in the matter of life after death for the pets we love.

A Special Relationship

"Animals have no souls as do people, and therefore when they die, their bodies simply return to the dust and that is the end of them."

That statement pretty well paraphrases the feeling of people who assign little value to the life and death of animals. While some of those who hold to this "cold-reality" viewpoint undoubtedly have had pets they loved dearly, I believe that the majority of people holding such a viewpoint have never allowed themselves to form emotional attachments to animals. Either their circumstances or their dispassion where emotional attachment to animals is concerned has prevented them from doing so. Most people who hold to this death-ends-all-life-for-animals view look at the animal world either in the most practical of terms (i.e., they are to serve for labor, food, etc.), or they regard them as just a notch above inanimate objects for the pleasurable human purposes they serve.

This assessment, as depressingly bleak as it is, can't be summarily dismissed as hateful cold-heartedness. Those who are less passionate about animals than we cannot prove their assertion any more than we who hold the opposite belief can prove ours. They can and do find and proclaim evidence for their beliefs, however; some of that evidence even comes from the Bible. Their contention usually begins with the book of wisdom, Ecclesiastes:

> For that which befalleth the sons of men befalleth beasts. Even one thing befalleth them: as the one dieth, so dieth the other…All go unto one place; all are of the dust, and all turn to dust again. Who knoweth the spirit of man that goeth upward, and the spirit of the beast that goeth downward to the earth? (Ecclesiastes 19–22)

Key to the argument that animals do not live again after death are these words: "who knoweth the spirit of man that goeth upward and the spirit of the beast that goeth downward to the earth?" Here, God's own truth tells that man's spirit doesn't remain in the ground, but that it goes upward at death, whereas the spirit of the animal being goes into the earth, where both man's flesh and the beast's flesh turn to dust. Therefore, it is obvious that man's spirit, his soul, lives eternally, while, when animals are taken in death, it is for them an act of finality.

Or, is this as obvious as it appears at first glance?

Is the Scripture here really saying that it's all over for the animal whose earthly life is finished?

. . . .

While leopards and lions are mentioned in Scripture, neither the word "cat" nor references to any type of domesticated feline appears in the Bible.

My basis for belief that we will again see the pets we love so much is also grounded in this Scripture, among others. Let's look at it again: "Who knoweth the spirit of man that goeth upward and the spirit of the beast that goeth downward to the earth?"

Note that both man and beast are linked by a common denominator: They both are beings that have *spirits*. Therefore, it is necessary to understand that there was from the very beginning a special relationship inalterably linking humankind and animals.

God tells us how and why the relationship between man and everything on earth, including the animal world, took place. The record is clearly laid out in the book of Genesis:

> And the LORD God said, It is not good that the man should be alone; I will make them an helpmeet for him. And out of the ground the LORD God formed every beast of the field, and every fowl of the air; and brought them unto Adam to see what he would call them: and whatsoever Adam called every living creature, that was the name thereof. And Adam gave names to all cattle, and to the fowl of the air, and to every beast of the field. (Genesis 2:18–20)

The Creator tells us that when He had made the animals, He cared for them very deeply and set about to see to their welfare. His deep involvement with these lowly creatures is crucial to note; man's involvement with the animals—man's love for the animal world—is the bind that seems to tie together the Creator with His two distinct created beings, man and animal. In His concern, God said:

> Let the earth bring forth the living creature after his kind, cattle, and creeping thing, and beast of the earth after his kind: and it was so. And God made the beast of the earth after its kind, and cattle after their kind, and everything that creepeth upon the earth after his kind: and God saw that it was good. (Genesis 1:24–25)

The Creator of all things continued His explanation of the all-important relationship, binding Himself to His creations, man and animal. His words, given here, form the foundation upon which I build my faith-based case that we as human beings and those pets we love with all our hearts are inseparable (and this is all-important)…IF WE CHOOSE NOT TO BE SEPARATED FROM THEM.

> And God said, Let us make man in our image, after our likeness; and let them have dominion over the fish of the sea, and over the fowl of the air, and over the cattle, and over all the earth, and over every creeping thing that creepeth upon the earth. So God created man in his own image, in the image of God created he him, male and female created He them. And God blessed them, and God said unto them, Be fruitful, and multiply, and replenish the Earth, and subdue it; and have dominion over the fish of the sea, and over the fowl of the air, and

over every living thing and over every living thing that moveth upon the earth. (Genesis 1:26–28)

Just as it is key to understand that God gave a *spirit* to the animals, so it is imperative that we believe Him when He says that He gave us—mankind—*dominion* over the animal kingdom. It is important, too, to understand and believe that God meant what He said when He informed us that He created us in His own image. Because that truth came from the Creator's own mind, we can be sure that He intended our ultimate destiny, our life after death, to include eternal power not unlike His own. To have dominion over a thing is to have power over it. In this truth resides the nucleus of the belief I hold, the strong trust I have that I will again be able to bear-hug my beloved old pal, Buckley, and feel his happy, wet kisses and playful bites in a very real, eternal world where time has no meaning and death is unknown. Buckley and I—together again!

chapter nine

Buckley

By Terry James

"When Buckley dies, please don't let me get another one," was my exact plea to Margaret, given in an only half-joking whine. Bulldogs are a constant demand on your life if you love them. And anyone who doesn't love a bulldog wouldn't have one long enough to know what a constant drain on your life they can be. Thus, the reason for the occasional ad in the classified section that reads something like "one-and-a-half-year-old bulldog, $200." That sort of ad always saddens me, but I understand it, without having to know the exact circumstances. When one has paid anywhere from five hundred to a thousand dollars for one of these fellows, and a year or so later is ready to sell him for two hundred bucks, those of us who are in love with the breed instantly know: This poor person didn't know what he or she was getting into when making the ill-fated investment.

Of course, knowing this doesn't keep us bulldog lovers from feeling great disdain for the person who placed the ad. Our usual comment is akin to, "How can anybody do that to a bully boy?" Bringing home a bulldog, you see, is, in our view, for keeps. For us, the time allowed with a bulldog by the Giver of All Life seems all too brief. We who are experienced know the heartbreak we court when we bring a bulldog into our lives; thus, the lament, "When Buckley dies, please don't let me get another one," was made more because of how much I knew it would hurt when death took him from us than because of the constant attention he required that took time away from other pursuits I would have preferred. The respiratory difficulties inherent in the breed; the almost-humanlike depression when bulldogs are separated from their human families for any length of time; the feeding problems they often endure because of swallowing difficulties— these things and more make it necessary that owners of bulldogs be a breed almost as special as the animals themselves.

This was how Buckley came to us:

When Butch left us that awful morning, the emptiness was cavernous. He had been my constant companion. He slept beneath my desk chair while I worked, enjoying the big fiberglass mat from which his hot bulky bulldog body absorbed coolness. He slept by the side of our bed at night. He sat with me while I watched television or did other things, and stretched across my lap during the height of the thunderstorms that often traverse our area.

Butch had cost us nothing except a tank or two of gas to go on "bulldog patrol" (see Butch's story, chapter 4) and the considerable veterinary expense that is a normal part of having a bulldog family member. Now he was gone, and I was in great pain. I was prepared to get or do whatever it took to relieve the aching empty spot that was with me every waking moment. Six hundred dollars seemed a reasonable amount to pay for even a slight bit of relief.

Margaret had been somewhat less attached to Butch than I had been. Nonetheless, she, too, was nearly as crazy with grief. And so we set about to buy yet another heartache in the making. A "beautiful red and cream little boy" was "just waiting for somebody to love him," the woman told us when we inquired about the puppy she listed for sale in the classified section of one of our dailies. "Sure, you can see him—just name the time," she told us that day. "How about now?" one or the other of us asked her on the phone.

It was, of course, love at first sight, the puppy performing for us on cue as the lady who owned him knew he would.

"Put him on the ground and show them how he greets you," the woman said to her husband, who smilingly did so. The eight-week-old puppy immediately fell over on his side while we approached him and began flailing his legs wildly at us, his beautiful brown eyes wide, a smile on his little mug, with his tongue dangling down. The closer we got, the more he wiggled. I'm glad they didn't ask ten thousand dollars for him at that moment, because if I had that amount to spend, I would have paid it.

Buckley continued to greet the family in exactly this fashion throughout his seven years with us whenever we had been away from him for more than a couple of hours. He always made us feel welcomed home.

Fat and happy, and seemingly a perfectly healthy puppy (although he, like all bulldog puppies up to a certain age, bore little resemblance to the wide, wrinkled, muscular folks they grow up to be), Buckley ate his puppy chow with enthusiasm. He seemed to enjoy his new home immensely, whenever we would leave him alone long enough to explore—a thing not easy to do when you are constantly held and loved by everyone in the family and by others who come by to see you. Still, Buckley was a good sport and returned the affection in every case.

· · · · ·

"We really don't know why this happens," our veterinarian said. "It looks like he has puppy septicemia," the doctor told us with great concern in his voice. "It's just one of those things we can't explain—maybe the change of environment and new germs… we just don't know."

Buckley was a very sick puppy, with high temperature and weakness that sometimes caused rigors and slight convulsions in his little body. The doctor's expression told us that Buckley was in serious trouble, although he gave us medicine and told us to let him know when there was a change. Nothing else could be done for him at the moment. The puppy grew worse, the bouts with the shivers coming more frequently. He wouldn't take food or water, though all of us gathered about him while he sat upon the softest pillow we could find, trying to convince him to take just a taste of puppy chow or an eye-dropper full of water. No matter how much any of us begged him, Buckley couldn't respond to our pleadings. Our hearts sank into depression, anticipating the worst, each of us praying silently in our own way for a miracle that I'm afraid none of us really believed would be granted.

The hours dragged by, and little Buckley just sat there and panted weakly, unable to lie down on his chest, probably because of respiratory problems. There was still hope however, because his brown eyes still glistened with life, and he still paid attention when we spoke to him.

You would have thought we had just won the Publisher's Clearinghouse Sweepstakes when Buckley suddenly accepted a dropper full of water, and then another, and then another. When we brought a small bowl of water to him, he lapped weakly at it and seemed to gain strength from doing so. He drank some more, and seemed to get even stronger, so we brought him the puppy chow, one pebble at a time, which he ate, somewhat reluctantly at first, then with increased vigor. We were elated, and continued feeding him by hand until he had had all he wanted. All the while we had to restrain ourselves from smothering him with love.

His remarkable recovery, I've always believed, was due to the direct intervention of the One who created him and to the invisible nurse—Buckley's angel—who must have hovered very near, desiring the little fellow's recovery every bit as much as we did.

Our veterinarian was genuinely surprised and visibly delighted when we brought Buckley back in to be checked over. It was obvious that he really hadn't expected the puppy to survive. "Oh yes," the doctor said. "This little man is doing much better," he concluded, much to our relief.

Buckley blossomed into full bulldoghood from that point, his chest widening, his forelegs and shoulders becoming heavily muscled, and his personality becoming more and more the stubborn, my-way-or-nothing, but totally lovable bulldoggedness appropriate to the male of his breed. Despite nostrils that were too narrow and nasal passages that presented problems with air passage (problems not unusual with this short-nosed breed) Buckley learned to "mouth breathe" after a time. But for a while following his close encounter with death as a puppy, he experienced bouts of respiratory congestion. Learning to mouth breathe snapped him out of it, the necessary exchange of air to his lungs and out again dissipating the congestion he previously suffered. All in all, Buckley grew up a healthy, very happy bulldog. But why shouldn't he? He had everything his own way around the James household.

Like Butch before him, Buckley was my constant companion, spending long hours at my feet beneath my desk chair on the cool floor mat. We shared special understanding on a level that I believe approached being spiritual in some ways. We often anticipated each other's movements. For example, he always seemed to know when I arose from my chair whether I was simply going to get a drink of water or whether I was going to take a nap. If a nap, then he was always right behind me on the way to the bedroom. He never missed an opportunity for a nap, and he preferred that I or someone else in the family be near him while he slept. I'm sure, however, that our almost-spiritual oneness had a lot to do with the fact that we were both creatures of habit and tradition. Buckley had his rituals; so did I—and more often than not, they closely coincided.

Buckley's favorite word was "bye-bye." The question, "Do you want to go bye-bye?" instantly infused his older, laid-back ways with energy like those days of his puppyhood. He happily bounded out the door and stood by the car awaiting us to open the door, at which time he would take his place on the front seat between Margaret and me, a seat that seemed to grow smaller with each "bye-bye." He loved to hang out of the window and feel the wind against his face while he stood on my legs with his elbows perched on the edge of the door.

When we took him to the store with us, usually on the cooler days, he stood on my lap while we waited in the car for Margaret for as long as her shopping trip took, and he watched every movement of the cars and people around. His silly face always brought broad smiles from those who passed by while we sat in the parking lot, and often people came up and asked the inevitable question, "Will he bite?" The answer, of course, was always, "He'll bite a biscuit if you've got one." Buckley was always incensed if people passed by without looking at him and saying something like, "How cute!" He never seemed to really approve of the common comment we often heard, "He's so ugly,

Did you know...? A dog's nose print is as unique as a human fingerprint!

he's cute!" But he always, nonetheless, accepted their pats on the head and acted happy to see them.

Buckley's least favorite words were, "How about a bath?" and "Let's cut those nails." These subjects always sent him into the hardest-to-reach corner he could find. Although he would never admit it—if he had the ability to admit it—a bath always perked him up, and trimming his big nails always made it easier for him to move about on the thick carpet. Like with us human family members who dreaded trips to the dentist, the anticipation of a bath or a manicure was for Buckley worse than the actual ordeal.

Besides the much-loved "bye-byes," Buckley's one consuming passion, his almost holy quest, was to spend as much time as he wanted on our bed. When I commanded that he not get on the bed, he reacted much like a frustrated child determined to get his way. This is the one area in which he and I had serious differences of opinion. As often as not, he would win the battle of wills, and I would acquiesce to his belligerent bulldog insistence that he be allowed on the bed. The words—"Get off that bed!"—were fighting words to Buckley, although he would get off after a few minutes of grumbling and groaning and tugging, then go sit in the corner and pout about it.

Every morning would find Buckley lying across my stomach, asleep, finally achieving his ultimate goal in life. When the bed had been freshly made up and neatly tucked, Buckley would inevitably launch himself onto the middle of it and we would often hear terrible growling, groaning, and snorting from our bedroom. We weren't alarmed, because we knew it was just our beloved bulldog at play. He would usually be on his back, his thick, stubby legs punching wildly at the ceiling while he wrestled with an imaginary something or the other that was, no doubt, in his bulldog mind, telling him to "get off that bed!"

Buckley didn't like the outside very much, probably because it was usually too hot, too cold, or because he didn't like the stickers that poked at his carpet-accustomed feet pads. Even the beautiful little girl bulldog named Tilly who lived across the street couldn't lure him from his comfortable home. Tilly sometimes bounded energetically over when she spotted Buckley. Buckley seemed to be somewhat put off by her forwardness and rolled his head from side to side on his thick neck to avoid her wet advances as she tried to lick his face and interest him in a game.

I will always believe that he gave up on girl bulldogs that morning in the veterinarian's office when we took him for some routine shots. While we were sitting there waiting, in pranced a beautiful female bulldog who stood with her human mommy while she gave the necessary information to the receptionist. Buckley walked up to Miss Bulldog and nuzzled her mug with his, put one of his muscular arms over her neck and licked her face. Instead of returning his affection, she pulled away from him and walked to a tall, handsome setter and affectionately nuzzled his shoulder. I really think that Buckley never got over that rejection.

The only girl animal in Buckley's life at this point was Samantha, our Manx, queen of all she surveyed. We knew Samantha loved Buckley very much, because if any other animal had chewed on her and wet her from the tip of her ears to the tip of her stub tail as did young Buckley, she would have quite literally torn its face off. With claws unlike any I had seen or have seen since, she was fully equipped to do so. Rarely did we see her discipline "her" bulldog, however, and when she did, it was usually with an insincere hiss and a gentle, quick slap with a sheathed claw front paw.

Buckley loved Samantha, too, and constantly badgered her to play during his very young puppy stage and later, in young adulthood, nipped her head and back with wet play bites when she passed near him. He seemed to understand and respect Samantha's need for rest and solitude during her elder years, and so sniffed and nudged her gently only when she obviously wished to nuzzle against him.

Buckley's seventh year of life with our family brought many happy moments, none more amusing than his dealings with a little gray cat dubbed Good Cat (GeeCee). Unlike her sister, Bad Cat, who was content to merely use Buckley as a rubbing post, as had all of Buckley's other cats, GeeCee saw in the big fellow much greater potential for fun and frolic. Any time Buckley stood around in our den to be near family activity, the kitten took full advantage of the opportunity to leap from a sofa or from the floor onto Buckley's back. While he tried in his nonflexible, bulldog sort of way to snap at her, she dug in all the harder, usually opening her mouth as wide as possible and chewing the back of his great neck, her ears pinned back and tail swishing, looking forevermore like one might expect a small leopard attacking a full-grown rhino to look. The cat would then switch ends quickly and attack his thick flanks, causing Buckley to swirl in an attempt to dislodge her. She was an amazingly good bulldog rider, and the spectacle is something we will never forget. The remembrance always brings a smile.

But, again, there is a time and a season for everything under Heaven. Change comes slowly or swiftly, but it comes, and it is not always welcome or pleasant, but such is the nature of earthly life. We move on. It is best when we can do so with a profound belief and trust that the Grand Designer will make it all come out for our best in His own good providence. Major changes came for us that Saturday evening when a roaring motor sound while Buckley sat by my side in the living room alerted us that something unusual had happened in one of the rooms off the hallway. Moments later, the house began filling with smoke—black, thick, and acrid. While neighbors ushered Buckley and the cats out of the house, Margaret dialed 911, and I hastily gathered crucial materials I had been working on from my desk.

A house fire, no matter how small, disrupts family life as perhaps few other disasters. Even if the burn damage is minor, smoke damage can, and in our case, did, require that the whole structure be stripped, cleaned, fumigated, and reconstructed on the inside. Samantha was no longer with us, but now Buckley and the other cats would spend many nights alone in a dark, cold, and fire-damaged house. Electricity and gas were the first casualties, required by city ordinances and regulations to be turned off until they could safely be used again.

Our animal family members were even more distressed and bewildered than were we. The cats, we were fairly certain, would be okay staying in the smelly though ventilated house. Buckley was another matter, so we consulted with our veterinarian, who told us that if there was any way possible, it would be best not to board him, because bulldogs often become quite stressed when in new surroundings away from those they love and trust. Buckley would most likely be okay, the vet told us, as long as the house remained cool. The lower humidity and temperature should neutralize any toxic fumes that might accumulate.

In retrospect, the reconstruction went quickly and smoothly, although at the time the whole thing seemed an endless ordeal for us and for our pets. But little Cala, our white Siamese motherly type, seemed to have things well under control, keeping the kittens and Buckley as comfortable as she could under the circumstances. I spent most of the days keeping Buckley company, and we often stayed as late as possible at night and always returned as early as we could in the mornings. When the reconstruction neared completion, Cala was struck and killed by a passing car early one morning.

Our gloom was thick and terrible, but if there was anything positive to be said, it was that Buckley, the kittens, and Felix were too disoriented from the fire and the disruption of their routine lives to so terribly miss Cala, as did we. Only Felix seemed to understand her passing; he had again stood by while Terry Jr. dug another grave in the corner of the yard.

The weather had been changing and the cool nights and pleasant early spring days had given way to the more typical heat and humidity of our region. Bulldogs don't fare well under such circumstances, so we moved him to a nearby motel, where the air conditioning could dispel the almost semitropical weather conditions Buckley would otherwise have to endure. At the time of orientation to his new surroundings, Buckley was able to relax and get back into his more normal sleeping pattern, although he was far from being his same old self. We didn't know how far until a few weeks later.

He was eating fairly normally, and he seemed more acclimated to the motel room and surrounding area, yet there was an ever-so-slight, but discernible, difference in his demeanor. By this time, the illness overtaking him caused a grouchiness much more severe than his normal, playful gruffness.

Repairs and renovations on the house had almost reached the point at which we could move back in and restore order to our household, human and animal. Our own nerves were pretty well frayed from the many weeks of having to live out of our element.

If your pet begins to choke, the Heimlich maneuver can save his or her life. First, position the pet: Lift a small pet so that the rear end is elevated higher than the head, and for large pets, reach over the back and raise the back of the legs. After positioning the pet, place your hands around the lowest part of the chest/upper abdomen, and give a quick, gentle thrust inward and upward. Gauge the force of the thrust to the size of the pet.

Grandma (my mother) very generously let us live with her, thus we avoided the necessity of living away from familiar surroundings. Margaret and I moved to the motel when Buckley could no longer stay in the hot, humid environment of our home, and the boys continued to live at their grandmother's for the last two weeks prior to our moving back home. But now things were looking up, and I wanted to reassure Buckley that soon his own little world would be put back together. Reasoning is the one form of communication we can't share with these marvelous little family members. If only we could make them understand...

It is easy to fail to realize, or to forget, that we look at the world from not only a mental perspective that includes reason, but from a physical perspective of elevation, whereas our small pets see everything at near-ground level. So it was with Buckley. He hadn't been in the house for several days while the construction crew recarpeted. Construction materials and debris taken out of the damaged interior filled the yard. Buckley didn't recognize that he was back home. The unfamiliar sights, sounds, and smells of the renovated interior seemed to confuse him, and it was disturbing to me that he didn't show the same old enthusiasm for rushing to the front door as soon as he got out of the car.

We shuffled still between the motel and our house, usually bringing Buckley with us, and he did begin to reestablish some familiarity with home. But now his health was changing more noticeably; his breathing was becoming more labored and occasionally his inhalations sounded as if he had croup. The rough, raspy sucking-in of air made my own throat tighten when I heard him. He then would breathe more normally for an extended period, and I thought maybe it was just a passing respiratory problem. Margaret and I agreed that as soon as we got back into the house, we must take Buckley to his doctor for a thorough checkup.

The house was finally completed to the extent that we could move in, and soon we had reestablished residence, but it was not the same even to us human family members. The cats seemed to love it, however, finding many new things to do with the renovations having provided new places to hide and new gadgets to explore and tinker with in the way only felines can. Buckley's bouts with labored breathing became more frequent, and he became increasingly nervous and restless because he was so uncomfortable. Although his (and our) bedroom was different, Buckley again claimed our room and bed as his own.

We didn't contest his determination to stay on the bed, because we knew he was feeling bad. Everything was still disorganized anyway, so we decided to let him have the bedroom while we slept elsewhere in the house until we could get things in better order. But he wanted to be close to us and followed us wherever we decided to sleep. Then he became markedly more distressed. His breathing became more rapid, a sure sign of distress—either emotional or physical, or both. He now seemed as if he were about to hyperventilate, and so we rushed him to the veterinarian.

Buckley, always happy to go to new places, went to the vet only on rare occasions, and so didn't recognize where he was until he caught the sights and sounds and smells of the waiting room.

Still, he displayed no signs of unhappiness over being there like he had on some of his trips to the doctor two years earlier. He seemed to be anxious to get into the examining room this time, and when I lifted him gently onto the steel examining table, he lay still and quiet, as if he knew this was all for his own good. Doctor Carol (we call her by her first name because she is not only our veterinarian but also a personal friend) looked him over carefully and listened to his chest, her look of concentration saying without words that she didn't like what she saw or heard.

"Sometimes smoke and fumes will cause or set up scarring in the lungs, and if this happens, there's really nothing we can do about it," she said. Her tone expressed concern rather than a cold, calculating clinical explanation. "Let's hope that that's not what has happened in this case. We'll give him some antibiotics."

Seven years of age is probably about average for the life span of a bulldog, at least a male bulldog. Many of the breed die much sooner of respiratory failure, heat stroke, or heart failure. People often forget the limits beyond which they should push their bulldogs in play or in exposure to excessive heat and humidity. But we had always been quite wary of his limitations and had taken care to stop strenuous activity before he became too fatigued or breathless. Buckley's care always foremost in our minds, we kept bowls of fresh water nearby at all times, and we never missed administering heartworm pills and other medication when needed. For the most part, he had been a healthy bulldog. Now, despite our care, despite our prayers, despite our wonderful veterinarian's medical expertise, Buckley was slipping from us.

Buckley's time was at hand, and he was beginning to suffer greatly—a thing we couldn't allow to go on for this little fellow who was, to us, our beloved animal child. His beautiful brown eyes no longer flashed with mischief, excitement, or curiosity; rather, now they showed apprehension and had in their quick, nervous glances a plea to those he trusted and loved to help him. And so, with as much courage as we could muster and with all the love in us, it was done.

It is impossible for me to think that this precious friend exists no more. The spirit within says otherwise, because Buckley's animal spirit, through my vivid and almost tangible memories of the time the Creator of all things allowed us to share on this Earth, remains real and springs dynamically to life anytime I choose to remember how very much he meant to us.

Strongheart, a German shepherd from, well, Germany, was quite the heartthrob among the canine set in the early days of the American cinema. He debuted in 1921 in the silent film, *The Silent Call*, a smash hit that opened the door for roles in many more films. Strongheart is one of three dogs (along with Lassie and Rin Tin Tin) to receive his own star on the Hollywood Walk of Fame.

chapter ten

Little Jack and Stanley

By Terry James

Two of our most cherished pets can't be left out of our treatment of *Do Our Pets Go to Heaven?* They are the most recent of our animal family members to have graced our lives, and among the pets who, for me, at least, are continually with me. One of them has departed this life, the other remains an every day, interactive part of my life while I do my work and other of life's activities.

First, about Little Jack...

"Oh no...you just take him back with you."

Margaret's words admonished Kiara, a little, exotically marked, mama cat with a tiny, orange kitten following behind. Kiara had brought the kitten several times. Margaret knew what she was up to, or at least, she told me she knew.

"She wants to leave that kitten here so we will take care of it."

"No," I said. "Definitely not going to do that. We don't need any more cats. We need to get rid of some of them," was my reply—which is always my response to a new cat anywhere near the James humble hovel.

We ended up with the equally exotically stamped "Little Jack," as we named him. He was so named because we already had a full-grown cat we had named "Jack." This one was brilliant orange, even more so than big Jack, so I suppose I thought he, too, looked like a Jack...probably for "jack-o-lantern" or something.

Little Jack fit right within the cat family, and I have come to think of him as probably one of the top two in intelligence of all our felines. At twelve years of age as of this writing, he remains an extremely smart cat, and among the most vocal. He will let you know when he wants something, and he has me, at least, trained to do his bidding.

Little Jack's story is another of the strangest of pet stories—strangeness that seems a part of our animals. What otherworldly relationship his particular story has to tell us, I'm not certain. But, there are some strange details indeed about the life of this bright orange feline with the crop-circle markings that make him easy to spot from half a block away, I'm told by those in the family who have eyesight—and that's everyone but me, as we have established.

Although there have been a number of unexplained things in Little Jack's life with us, the strangest of all came about at a time when he had been with us for six or seven years.

We started hearing all kinds of squawking from a mockingbird—the one brand of bird most prevalent in Arkansas. As a matter of fact, the mockingbird is the official state bird. This mockingbird was squawking, so we thought a cat had the bird, or one of the bird's young, and the distressed bird was raising a ruckus.

(Sadly, our cats are like all others. They kill anything they can get. And they perform almost supernatural gyrations to make such kills. Like, when Harry, our Maine Coon cat of about twenty-two pounds, leapt seemingly supernaturally high in the air from a flat-footed position in the backyard to miss knocking down a harassing blue jay by only an inch. The jay seemed totally in awe of that huge cat almost reaching him. It went and perched on a high fence and looked at Harry, not moving for a long time. I'm convinced it was thinking, "That thing thinks it can fly. I had better cool it.")

> For your pet's sore or runny eyes, rinse with saline eye drops every four hours until the eyes are clear.

So, Margaret rushed outside to see if she could save the mockingbird she thought surely was about to go to its reward. She watched as the squawking mockingbird hovered just about Little Jack's back, touching him lightly with its claws. Strangely, Little Jack just kept walking calmly, paying little attention to the harassing bird.

Little Jack kept walking up the street by the curb. Soon, the bird landed right beside him, no more than a few inches, still chirping. Margaret and several others watched this spectacle for several minutes. Little Jack looked at the bird, and the bird at him, and the cat walked calmly, while the bird hopped, as mockingbirds do, beside him on the asphalt.

The onlookers were astonished—and Margaret, at least, was concerned that Little Jack would snatch it at any moment. That cat and bird walked along without so much as a seeming concern for any tensions that should be between them.

For weeks, the mockingbird would chirp in a distinctive chirp from across the street on a rooftop, on a tree, on a car nearby. It would come and sit on the ledge of our front window, or hover and flutter, looking in, chirping, if Little Jack was lying on the sofa back looking out.

Margaret would open the door, Little Jack would go outside, and that little bird would come and either flit around over him or land beside him. They were pals—there was no other explanation we could think of.

We often have wished we had filmed those many minutes of interplay between the cat and the bird. It would have been of most interest to animal behaviorists or to YouTube.com viewers.

This went on for months. The winter came, and the little mockingbird wasn't back the next spring. We want to believe that a cat didn't get it; we know for sure that Little Jack didn't hurt it.

Our other cats, I would never vouch for in that regard.

What it did set me to thinking about is what the millennial kingdom, reigned over by Jesus Christ, will be like. The lion will eat grass, the bear and the lamb will lie down together, and the child will put his or her hand in the cobra's hole and not be harmed. Being lovers of animals, we certainly look forward to that time of complete restoration of the way things were before the debacle in Eden.

I think that Heaven demonstrated just a little of what will one day be when Little Jack and that little mockingbird were at complete peace with each other. I believe they will again be best pals.

· · · · ·

Now, about Stanley, from my heart.

Stanley coming into my life and the life of my family is perhaps the most significant of all personal pet memories. It is a remembrance I will take with me until I depart from this troubled sphere. I believe I will, for the first time, look upon this very special little feline in that grand reunion all who enter the heavenly realm ultimately enjoy.

Stanley and I almost never met. This is, in a way, the strangest of our family's pet stories. His and my meeting was a get-together that had to be predestined, preordained by the Power on High.

My strangely wonderful get-together with Stanley really began, I believe, the afternoon of Good Friday, April 22, 2011. It was a pivotal day in my life.

As was my usual routine, I worked out in the afternoon, doing a series of exercises I had basically done for physical fitness reasons since sometime in 1979, when I had lost the ability to see well enough to work in my job as public relations director for a local company. The job had required that I be able to drive and do other things that depended upon good eyesight, and my vision, by that year, had deteriorated to the point that I could no longer do so. I left my job with the company and began doing freelance writing jobs in the same field, but without the travel previously required.

So, to maintain my health and make up for the new, more sedentary, lifestyle, I began a routine of physical exercise that continued until that fateful day in 2011. By this time, I had become totally blind.

That afternoon, I had finished the nearly two-hour workout and was using the recumbent bicycle for a cool-down of fifteen minutes or so. When finished, I felt pressure in my chest and a burning sensation. It grew worse until I was having trouble breathing. I had never had a really serious sick day to this point in my life —sixty-eight years old at the time. I thought that I was just having an unusual case of indigestion, and that it would soon go away.

It didn't. Soon my wife had called 911 for an ambulance, and I was on my way to the hospital, about two miles from our home.

The medics in the ambulance reported that I was having a coronary. A coronary! Me?! Just couldn't be!

But, it was me having a heart attack, and my chest felt as if

. . . .

A close look at pets' eyes: It's long been thought that cats and dogs only see in black and white; however, researchers say that is a myth. A cat's eyes are larger than those of any other meat eater; and as far as visual acuity, surprisingly, neither fares very well—both rely more on motion than on focus and both are quite farsighted.[16]

it would explode, so great was the pressure. Within minutes the medics were pulling the gurney, with me on it, out of the back of the van.

The pain and pressure built to the point I thought my chest would explode. I heard a strange *blip* sound—like a computer makes when going from one website to another on the Internet.

I was instantaneously standing before a throng of young, cheering men and women—probably no older than twenty-five years of age. They were cheering and beckoning me to join them.

I didn't think about where I was or where I had come from—just that I was here, and it was all spectacularly beautiful. I never wanted to leave.

My surroundings again turned totally dark, and I was back on the gurney as they were rushing me through the hospital to the cath lab, where they would begin the procedures to try to save my life.

One young man said he had to hit me with the defibrillation paddles. My heart had stopped. In fact, my heart failed two more times inside of those forty-five minutes, while the doctors worked on me to remove the blockage to a major artery. It was a "widow-maker" heart attack, they had told my wife. They didn't think they could save me.

Each time the pressure built in my chest and my heart stopped, I stood before that same crowd of young folks. Each time was more spectacular than the previous. Each time I didn't want to leave that realm.

Back in the cath lab after the third episode of my heart stopping, the blockage was removed, the stent was implanted to assure blood flow, and I'm thankful to say, I haven't had a moment's trouble to this point of writing.

Margaret is a cat fancier, which we've already solidly established in this book. And, I must admit that I, as you've already read, kind of like them, too. So it was when a little girl rode up on her bicycle with a little yellow cat draped across her bicycle's handlebar that Margaret agreed, although not immediately, to take it in. The girl said she wasn't allowed to keep it.

This is where Heaven intervened. I was sent a furry, little helper in my ongoing recovery from my near-death adventure, as I now like to call it. My "seeing-eye cat" had arrived! He was delivered by a little angel on a bike.

That was our introduction to Stanley. He was, as I said, yellow, with short fur, and with a personality like none other we can remember.

Stanley would stare at you, the family said. It was as if he was studying us, analyzing us. While most of the felines would do cat things, Stanley's specialty seemed to be observing human beings.

Soon he took up with me. Like Clifton Webb in the movie *Cheaper by the Dozen* said in his curmudgeonly way about a full-grown dog the family wanted to adopt, "He will attach himself just to me. They always do."

Stanley did stick to me. From day one, I was his personal project, and that is an understatement.

The other cats have learned to stay out of my way. Because of my blindness, many a tail has been stepped on as I shuffle down the hallway as one of them or the other is munching from a bowl of cat food, with their tails sticking out from beneath the piano.

Stanley, from the first day he lived with us, would stick with me no matter where I moved in the house. He would get in front of my left foot and leg. He would bump against me, trying to get me to slow down, while he led me down the hallway.

Everyone in the household would watch his service as a lead cat for the blind. This happened every time I got up from my chair or walked from my office: Stanley would be right there, guiding me, walking in front of me, bumping against my left ankle—to control my movement, I'm sure he thought. He would get up out of a sound feline sleep just to do his duty.

Once I got to where I was going, I would always pick him up and pet him and tell him what a good boy he was.

If I was in the bathroom, he would wait right outside the door, no matter how long it took. He would then use his technique of bumping against the leg to lead me back to wherever I ended up.

I believe that Stanley knew I was blind, and it was Heaven's way of letting me know that he was especially sent, through that little girl on the bicycle, to serve as a source of love and amusement—as well as to assist an old blind guy in negotiating the hallway and other places.

Stanley was with us almost two years. My friend Todd—my partner in our prophecy website, raptureready.com, and who also is my neighbor—called me one morning to tell me the terrible news.

"One of your cats has been hit by a car," he said. "It's one of the yellow ones."

My heart sank, because we have several and love them all. I just never thought it would be Stanley—this special little friend that had been delivered by Heaven's courier service less than two years earlier.

I still just sometimes say in a whisper to myself, for no reason whatsoever, his name—"Stanley." One eternal day, when I'm in that magnificent realm among those young folks to stay, I believe I'll say that name, and I will see him for the first time. We will never be parted again.

Stanley apparently isn't the only "seeing-eye cat"; an eight-year-old dog, Terfel, largely immobile because of cateracts, was "rescued" from his sedentary lifestyle by a stray cat his owner took in. The owner says she "watched as the cat approached Terfel, and led him out of confinement and into the garden," and she marveled at the way the feline—now quite the Internet celebrity—used her paws to guide the dog and keep him out of harm's way.[17]

chapter eleven

Sprout and BlackJack
Does God Care about Animals,
and Does He Still Use Them?

By Allie Anderson

We had made the decision: We were leaving the city.

It was time to get to a more rural state of life for the sake of our children. We sold most of our belongings and our home—all but one small pickup and one RV. What didn't fit in the back of the pickup, the small trailers being pulled by the pickup and the RV, or in one of the seats was "sold" at a garage sale (meaning that by the end of the day, we were giving things away just to keep from having to find a place to haul them).

So there we were—my husband, our ten-year-old son, our five-year-old daughter, and our two-year-old black lab, Sprout.

We set off, intending to live in the RV until we found just the perfect destination to make a new life for our kids. It was the kind of adventure that caused everyone we knew to either look at us with envy, often saying they wished they had the means or the nerve to do such a thing, or to look at us like each of us had just hatched a second head. Those looks were often followed by a vague nod, with no further conversation.

On the way to our destination, we began to notice that our black lab, Sprout, was beginning to slow down in her negotiation of the RV steps. She started acting strangely, sometimes lethargic and carsick—very unlike the dog always so quick to jump into the car for a trip to anywhere "her kids" (meaning our daughter and son) were headed. When her stomach began to swell, we put two and two together...

Oh no...

We remembered that day we were working on the yard and that mastiff from up the street kept hanging around. Sprout was in heat, so we had been keeping a sharp eye on her, but there was that ten-minute span when she had gotten out.

We had yelled for her frantically, with me saying under my breath, "Oh please, God, no...not when we're about to move! Don't let this dog get pregnant now!"

Then she had come bounding toward us, acting like everything was fine, and, with a sigh of relief, in the frenzy of our move, the entire event had been forgotten.

Until now.

Sprout, a "Christmas puppy," had been named for the brussels sprouts she had somehow gotten hold of her first night in the house. Our daughter, who was three at the time, claimed innocence in this matter. Dubious at her innocence, my husband and I stated that it must be our good fortune to have acquired a puppy of such intelligence that she was able to, with no help at all from "her kids," open the refrigerator, get into the produce drawer, pull out a bag of brussels sprouts, close the produce drawer, shut the door to the fridge, and then proceed to pull out each brussels sprout and chew it up completely, leaving the little, mangled, hard balls all over the floor for me to find the next morning. And what a crafty dog not to have even torn the produce bag when she removed each sprout all by herself, with no help from our preschooler!

Fast forward to just a few weeks after we embarked on this adventurous move that involved my family of four plus what I thought would be only one dog living in an RV. I was staring at twelve puppies just as cute and rambunctious as Sprout had been at their age. (It was bad enough when I had thought there were only ten puppies. How would I ever place that many puppies into homes in a community where I

> If your dog gets burrs in his or her fur, rub vegetable oil on your fingers and work the lubrication through the fur until you can pull the burrs out. For cats, who typically prefer to do their own grooming, work the burrs through with a wire brush.

didn't know anyone, and how—oh, how—would we all live in this RV together? But Sprout, after delivering ten, had gone outside for her favorite activity, fetch, with "her girl" who was now five years old, and, when the new mama went back inside to lay with her newborn pups, to our shock, she delivered two more!)

Twelve puppies!

(Didn't Disney make a cartoon about this?)

Well, on our way during this adventure, we parked the RV at my parents' house to visit with them for a few days. From time to time, we opened the trailer to dig around for things we needed— a tool or an item of clothing, etc. After we concluded our visit, we hit the road to see my husband's parents, all the while scoping out the communities at both places and in between for potential places we might settle down. While we were cruising down the freeway, however, the RV tire blew. What a bummer.

My husband pulled the vehicle to the side of the road safely, and immediately, I started doing one of the things I do best: panicking. I wasn't bashful about voicing my concerns, and I began firing off a list of them:

"How can you jack up this huge RV?"

"Do you even have a spare?"

"Do they make tow trucks big enough to pull this?"

"Where would we even tow it to…and how much will it cost?"

As usual, my husband downplayed our trouble, being as prepared as he always is. He simply shrugged and let me know that, of course, he had a jack; yes, indeed he had planned ahead and made sure the spare was in place; and yes, he could take care of

. . . .

The health benefits of having dogs as companions have been backed by research for more than twenty-five years. Dogs have been shown to do everything from reduce stress and lower blood pressure to prevent depression and even boost immunities.[18]

this right here on the side of the road. We would be on our way within the hour.

When he opened the trailer to retrieve his tools, to our complete surprise, out jumped my mom's cat, Kino! Now, Kino had already had such a journey that had led her to my sister's house in the first place (and then later to my mother's) that her reputation as a traveler had already been well established. Evidently, she had jumped in when we weren't looking—probably during one of those times when we had been digging around for something.

My husband, as usual, made short work of our car troubles, and we were on our way, with one detour: heading back to my mom's to return her cat.

What I have failed to mention was that our plan involved parking these trailers at my husband's parents' house for an undetermined length of time while we continued to decide where to settle. God only knows how long the cat would have been in that trailer—without food, water, and good ventilation. The outcome couldn't possibly have been good for the cat.

I wondered at how funny life can be sometimes. What I initially panicked about—the flat that had caused a delay in our trip, and that could have been very expensive and possibly even dangerous—worked out just fine. Turns out, we were protected and in God's hands the whole time. As I considered the bigger picture, I realized it had all happened…for whom? A cat! God cared so much about that cat that He intervened so we could discover Kino in time to save her life.

Fast forward three years.

We had moved out of the RV and into a house, and had gone

about our lives. Sprout, unfortunately and devastatingly (especially to our daughter), had since been hit by a car and killed.

One of her puppies, however—BlackJack, as my son named him for his sleek black coat—was still with our family. We had managed to find homes for the eleven others, but BlackJack had stayed. With all the qualities of a lab—playful, loyal, and loving—plus all the protective qualities of his mastiff daddy now so far away, he loves "his kids," being especially protective of "his girl." She, in turn, loves him deeply and the two are inseparable. BlackJack sleeps where our daughter sleeps, sits where she sits, and meets her at the bus stop each day like clockwork.

That winter, however, our daughter caught rotavirus and became very, very sick very, very fast. Nine days went by with her being unable to keep down so much as water, and her complexion took on a dangerous shade of gray that no mother ever wants to see on her child. Ever.

She had to have three IVs during this week just to rehydrate, and a large part of what ended up saving her life was an anti-nausea topical cream that was rubbed onto her belly so that she could at least keep water down—because she couldn't even tolerate the anti-nausea drugs that were originally prescribed. We were in and out of the emergency room several times during that period, although she was never admitted to the hospital for overnight stays.

During this time, the entire family had to make major adjustments in order to accommodate my daughter's illness. So that I could be by her side night and day, we unfolded the hide-a-bed couch to convert the living room into "our room." Of course, no one else was allowed to make noise in this room or do anything to disturb her rest. Smells would launch her into uncontrollable vomiting, so we stopped cooking; instead, we switched to eating sandwiches, apples, and anything else that didn't require cooking or stir up even the slightest aroma during their preparation. Further, I wasn't always able to eat, because she didn't want me to leave her side. And beyond that, to eat anything even near her triggered the horrendous nausea, causing her to lose any precious fluid she might be keeping down. When she fell asleep every now and then, and never for more than a half hour or so, I would sneak away and try to eat, drink, and shower. I spent all the other moments of the day by her side, praying intently the entire time. It was scary and exhausting.

During this entire week, BlackJack became a different dog. Obviously aware that something was very wrong, he wouldn't leave her side. I literally had to grab his collar and drag him outside just to go potty—and even doing that, I could only get him to go once a day. He didn't want to eat, either. He would sit next to a full food bowl and scratch at the door, insisting that he wanted inside—near his girl—more than he wanted food. He didn't want to go run and play. He didn't want to drink. He just sat glued to her side the entire week.

By about the fifth or sixth day of our daughter's illness, my body was becoming so exhausted that when she would stir, I wasn't waking up as quickly as I had in the beginning. I knew she needed me, and I wanted to be there every moment that she needed me, but the physical exhaustion of having little to no sleep, rare opportunities to eat or drink, combined with the heightened anxiety of the situation had begun to take its toll.

At that point, BlackJack began to do something he had never done before and has never done since. (I hope he never needs to do it again.) He took on an insistent strength. His casual, easy-to-please demeanor was replaced with an authoritative, purposeful countenance. Although he couldn't speak with words, his intent showed through his actions. He would, at times during the day, jump up and stand next to her, looking at me as if to let me know I needed to investigate. She was so weak that sometimes I had to try to figure out what she needed without her telling me. It was almost like caring for an infant who cannot tell you what the problem is. If I hadn't figured out what she needed, BlackJack would keep staring at me with that purposeful look in his eyes until, eventually, I would figure it out. Then he would lie at her feet again, where he spent that entire nine-day period.

If his "girl" needed something at night, BlackJack would come around to my side of the hide-a-bed and ram my face with his nose until I woke up. He has never been a dog to do that before or since. And when I did awaken, he would quickly run around the bed to her side, and stand next to her again with that insistent look in his eyes.

Whether I was awake or asleep, I had another watcher making sure I didn't miss a time when she needed something. I have never been so thankful for a dog shoving a wet nose in my face repeatedly while I was trying to sleep. He watched over her like a guardian angel. I don't think he slept that entire period. I know he didn't eat.

Finally, one day she woke up and asked for food. It was still a few more days before she was able to keep it down, but the upswing had begun. When the dangerous time was over, Black-Jack stopped that behavior and went back to being his usual, easy-to-please, mopey self. He has never nudged his face against mine in my sleep again.

I have always known that he is a huge part of the reason we still have our little girl.

It all started with Sprout, his mother, connecting with our little girl all alone that night with the brussels sprouts, but the relationship still lives through BlackJack to this day.

Did you know they were female? Toto's role in *The Wizard of Oz* was played by a female Cairn Terrier named Terry, and the Taco Bell dog is actually a female Chihuahua named Gidget.[19]

chapter twelve

Tiny

By Carl Anderson

I am alive today due to a dog.

I grew up on the high plains in Wyoming. We owned a forty-seven-acre ranch outside of the city of Pavillion. It was as beautiful as that area gets: buffalo grass and prickly pears. The backdrop of the Pavillion mountain formation was breathtaking, though.

Most ranchers wanted to raise cattle, but the weather was so tough in the 1970s, when I was a boy, that many cattle farmers had tremendous losses and converted to raising sheep, which are very resilient creatures. Sheep appear to be small, fluffy, and sweet-tempered, but I can tell you that, like any animal, they will take on the temperament of their owner, and they will act according to how they are treated.

Since growing up and leaving the area, I have really thought about the culture in Wyoming during that time. I think a difficult environment breeds a difficult people. Our neighbor was one of those very difficult people. Every time his sheep came onto our property, according to him, we were the ones to blame.

One evening, our neighbor's sheep once again got onto our property. To prevent another reprimand, our parents sent us kids out to herd the animals back onto his land. I was just five, and didn't weigh more than sixty pounds soaking wet. Being the youngest of that group of working kids, I didn't get a horse.

What I did get was Tiny.

Tiny was an Irish wolfhound who weighed about 160 pounds. His tail had destroyed more of my mother's drinking glasses than any of her nine kids. I was the middle child, so I watched Tiny help raise at least three children.

He was huge! He had a monstrous tongue that could lick a kid clean in one swipe. And he was so gentle and tolerant: The little ones in my family would tug on his ears, pull his fur, and even drag that giant tongue out of his mouth.

But, I digress; I'll get back to the story. The memory of an old savior brings him back.

It was just beyond dusk so you couldn't see clearly; everything was in purples. We had already engaged the herd and had herded them right up against the break in the fence.

My job as "ground crew" was to move the barbed wire out of the way so the sheep could get out. Then we would repair the fence.

A very stubborn ewe would not move to allow me to do my

job. So, I put my size-4 boot to her butt. I heard my brothers yell—it was a yell of desperation and importance! I turned, and saw Tiny in a way I had never seen him before. He was coming right at me, but not with his usual mouth open, slobbery, lazy gait. His mouth was closed, he was moving with everything he had in him!

He wasn't coming to play or for a gentle nuzzle. He wasn't even looking *at* me; he was looking *through* me!

What happened next I'll never forget: Tiny jumped! He passed cleanly *over* my head. I heard a *thump* behind me, and turned around to see the neighbor's ram. A huge, two-hundred-pound animal (remember, I was just five; that's *huge!*) with dirt-caked, curled horns was pinned on its back underneath Tiny.

My perspective on this story is limited due to my stature and age. But my brothers, who had a different vantage point from horseback, told me they had seen the neighbor's ram set his sights on me and dig his hooves in, starting a run for an incredible butt right to my cerebral cortex.

When Tiny did what he did, he saved my life. This always reminds me that God has a plan for me! I pray I live up to His expectations. It makes me feel humble that He would send such a noble creature into my life to extend it.

. . . .

Greyhounds can run as fast as 45 mph, and are the fastest canines on the planet.[20]

If your dog has a run-in with a skunk, make a solution of one quart hydrogen peroxide, ¼ cup of baking soda, and 1 teaspoon liquid soap. Work the solution into the fur (avoiding eyes), then rinse. If odor lingers, drench your dog in tomato juice and leave the solution on for several minutes before rinsing. Repeat if needed.[21]

chapter thirteen

Lurch
My Dog Chose Me

By Kat (age 12)

You may have chosen your dog or cat, but I did not. My dog, Lurch, chose me.

We got my dog from a friend who lived a little ways down the street. She had at least twenty-five dogs. The woman had rescued dogs that she found. She was giving away dogs because she could not pay to feed them all, and could not bear to set them free and hope they live or see them put down.

As she was telling my parents and me about the dogs, I looked behind myself to see that Kong (the name of Lurch *before* we got him) was slowly following me. The first thing I saw was he was poorly fed and weak, which is why he was slow. So I paused to pet him. He loved all my attention a lot.

Then I went to catch up with the group, and before too long, I saw Kong again. This repeated a few times.

In my family, I am the one who picks the animals because I love on them, feed them, and take care of them the most. When it came time to choose which dog I wanted, I chose Kong because he chose me. He is named Lurch now because he looks like Lurch off of *The Adams Family*.

I still know he chose me, because any room I go in, he is there to protect me.

It's hard to find a dog who's more famous or more firmly planted in pop culture than snoopy, Charlie Brown's pal. After creator Charles M. Schultz passed away in 2000, the comic strip featuring Snoopy and the rest of the Peanuts gang was being printed in 2,600 newspapers in seventy-five countries and twenty-one languages.[22]

chapter fourteen

Rin Tin Can

By Nita Horn

Many people of different races, creeds, and religions have speculated at one time or another what Heaven is like. Perhaps you have marveled at the thoughts of streets of solid silver and gold. Others may ponder whether these fine metals are tangible elements that are important to our soul, or if they're merely a glittery glimpse of things to come in the afterlife...

What is Heaven, anyway? I believe it is a place of peace where there are no more tears, no sadness, no pain, and no suffering—a place that, when we really open our minds to think about, comforts us with the thought of dearly departed loved ones, with big Cheshire-cat smiles and open arms, waiting for our arrival at its gate.

I have personally found consolation in these thoughts many times when reflecting upon the reality of the sudden death of my little sister who was taken from this earth by a car accident at the tender age of eleven. Beatrice Althia was my best friend, and even though several decades of time have passed since her death, I still think of her often and miss her to this day. And I have always believed that she *is* standing at Heaven's gate cheering me on, along with a plethora of those who have gone before us: those whose memories of them remind me to keep the faith so that we will one day be reunited through the sacrificial blood of Jesus Christ.

But...what about our pets? What happens to them when they leave this world? Do animals become nonexistent, or do they have an eternal existence in the afterlife?

What about my faithful companion at age nine: an adorable, lanky-legged, black Labrador named Jake, my favorite dog in the world who followed me everywhere I went up until the day he was gone? Or how about this other buddy of mine: a stunted buckskin pony named Ol' Shorty—whatever became of him? As a young teen, I told Shorty every secret an adolescent girl could hold in her heart; he listened, and quickly became my best friend. Unlike other girls my age, I never needed a diary, because I had Shorty. He never talked back, and he always agreed with me (that is, as long as I brought him a bucket of grain).

But, of course, I will never forget a special little pup my dad had named "Rin Tin Can." It was late one afternoon on a sum-

- -

Dogs sweat through the bottoms of their feet and they discharge heat by panting.

mer day. My sister and I were playing. Suddenly, we heard Mom shouting. Her voice echoed through our room as a bloodcurdling "doggie" yelp simultaneously pierced our ears.

"RINNY!" she cried.

We looked wide-eyed at each other, our jaws dropped, and our stomachs sank. We knew something was terribly wrong. My sister was right on my heels as we ran out to see what was happening. Upon arriving at the scene of the incident, we gasped and clasped our hands over our mouths in disbelief.

There, lying helpless on the ground in the middle of the driveway, was our silly little bug-eyed, pug-nosed, long-haired, shaggy, red dog we lovingly called Rin Tin Can (a parody version of the popular name from my dad's old favorite 1960s TV program, *Rin Tin Tin: K-9 Cop*).

Rin Tin Can ("Rinny," for short) was a far cry from that gallant celebrity German shepherd in all his Hollywood glory. Our dog only weighed about ten pounds soaking wet, hair and all, and was as ugly as a mud pie. We always said he was so ugly that he was cute! I'm quite sure he would have been a great contender in the World's Ugliest Dog competition.

(I cannot for the sake of my life recall where he even came from. Dad was always bringing home free puppies and stray dogs. He didn't care what they looked like; he was an equal-opportunity stray dog finder and collector. He had a soft and bleeding heart for dogs. Of course, we kids loved this kind quality about Dad, and always looked forward to the next family addition, but Mom was not so favorable toward her husband's unique characteristic.)

Although Rinny was funny to look at, in no time he had somehow won our hearts and had become a part of the family. He even did tricks! He would sit up, beg, and lay down…even my mom became "sweet" on Rinny (and "lay down" was Mom's favorite of his tricks).

Unfortunately, tragedy is no respecter of person or animals, and calamity was looming that day when my sister and I ran outside to see about the commotion. You see, Rinny was a pretty smart dog, except for one dumb habit we couldn't break him of: He loved to sleep snugly underneath the back tire of our cars. I can't tell you why; I suppose the warmth from the car exhaust provided a comfortable place to rest. Usually when the motor would start, he would wake up and wiggle his way out just before the car began moving.

On this particular day, however, Rinny must have been extra tired. Apparently, he hadn't heard the Chevrolet Corvair motor starting. And, instead of moving forward, Dad had slipped the car into reverse.

"Vrooom, vroom, clunk, shpew!" The tires had rolled back as Dad backed out over the top of the lazy little sleeping beauty. To Dad's surprise, the car ker-blumped over something as he heard a loud yelp and my mother screaming the dog's name.

"It was bound to happen," my mom said after the initial shock had settled. Dad was sad to admit the inevitable. My sister and I were devastated! This was *Rin Tin Can*… the fearless hero dog! Nothing could hurt Rinny! Until that moment, we had been certain that silly dog would be with us forever.

Well, Mom gently placed Rinny in a cardboard box and took

him into a nearby shed to die in peace. But after a little while, she couldn't stand the idea of this poor helpless creature suffering any longer, so she decided the humane thing to do would be to help end his agony. She went to the medicine cabinet and took a handful of aspirin (about fifteen or so), ground them up, put the powder into an eye dropper, and inserted the medication into his mouth, forcing him to swallow. Her intent was to send him into a permanent, peaceful sleep.

We were distraught that Mom would do this; if the car didn't kill him, surely those aspirin would!

In either case, my sister and I did the only thing we knew to do. We went back to our room to mourn the death of this tiny, fuzzy family member. We decided to pray to God for a miracle of mercy: *"Please, spare his life oh Lord! He's our little-bitty doggie…Please don't let Rinny die!"*

> If your dog has itchy skin, put rolled oats into a stocking and drop it into a tub full of warm water. Soak him or her in the water for ten to fifteen minutes. (Not recommended for cats.)

The whole time I wondered if God, the Creator of the universe, would actually hear the prayers of two small, insignificant girls. And would He concern himself over a dog? *Really?* After all, *He* certainly had a great, big world to run, angels to command, and so many other more important tasks on His plate. Nevertheless, the rest of that day we interceded and travailed in prayer for the life of our Rinny. We had nothing else to lose, so we continued on in our faint attempt at faith, until we both fell asleep.

Early the next morning, we both ran out to check on Rinny. I must admit, I did have a spark of hope that maybe, just *maybe*, God had heard and answered the cries of two helpless girls who loved their doggie so much. The evidence of the day before seemed to overshadow that hope, but we still ran out to the shed to investigate.

To our surprise, there was Rinny sitting up in the cardboard box, rocking back and forth on his front legs, trying to reach us to let us know he was still there and had been given a second chance! It was nothing short of a miracle. It was God allowing us to know for the first time in our young lives that He *does* hear the prayers of little people, and He *does* care for our pets!

I still get choked up thinking about how God made Himself real to us that day. He became more than a Sunday-school lesson…He *was* real, and He had heard us. He had heard *me!* He had granted our petition to allow our pup to remain with us for a time. I have never stopped believing that God Almighty, up above in His huge kingdom, overseeing all the interactions of the ceaseless universe, has time and concern for a little girl and her doggie.

He *still* hears me when I talk to Him…and I do talk to him, and he *still* cares.

Because of his injuries, Rinny dragged his back end around for a few weeks, but he slowly began walking again with only a slight limp, which served as a reminder of his bout with death and an answered prayer. He has passed on since, and although he is no longer on this earth, I know he is standing right at my sister's feet, right there next to Jake, and yes…by even Ol' Shorty, too, waiting for the rest of us to join them in Heaven!

Rin Tin Tin, a German shepherd born in France in 1918, became a canine movie star in America after he was brought to Los Angeles and trained by his owner, US Air Corporal Lee Duncan, after the war. Once he caught the eye of a movie producer and was given roles in *Where the North Begins* and *Man from Hell's River*, he became a film sensation, going on to make twenty-six more films as well as star in his own live radio show, *The Wonder Dog.*[23]

chapter fifteen

The Animals and Us

By Terry James

Animals have been a part of fulfilling America's Manifest Destiny—a term I make no apology for using, although today it is criticized as a term of shame by some. America has proven to be made up of people who have helped others around the world, whenever and wherever disasters strike and great needs arise. So, it is without apology that I view this country as one that indeed was given a mission to accomplish by the Creator of all things. We have failed greatly many times, because America is made of human beings with human weaknesses. But, it has been a nation of unprecedented generosity and accomplishment for the good of mankind.

The farm animals and even the pets of those pioneers over the several centuries of the settling of the continent have contributed mightily to achieving the blessings we enjoy today. And, in turn, the nation has blessed the world in many ways.

Our young men—and many women—have given their lives to save others in wars that dictators started, intending to enslave people, if not stopped. Animals have, on many occasions, accompanied the soldiers who gave up hearth and home in order to serve in foreign places.

At the same time, animals have served alongside humans in many societies and cultures around the world. They have in many cases performed truly astounding feats. The following are excerpts recounting the bravery of some of those furry heroes.

Tang Saves Lives

In 1919, a Canadian steamer, *Ethie*, was transporting cargo and crew off the West Coast of Newfoundland. Aboard the ship was a Newfoundland dog named Tang. Newfoundlands, known for their strong swimming skills and intelligence, were often used as work animals in European and American ships.

On the night of December 10, while the ship and crew were heading towards Bonne Bay, a winter blizzard came up. By the

. . . .

The most popular pet in America is...FISH! That's because of the sheer numbers involved in fish ownership (most people have one or two dogs and/or cats, whereas fish lovers have aquariums full of their beloved finned creatures). However, if you take fish out of the equation, the list of most popular pets is headed by dogs. Cats come in at a close second, followed by birds, small animals, horses, and reptiles.[24]

next morning, the cargo on the decks was lost; the lifeboats—or what was left of them—were destroyed; and the entire ship was covered in ice. Captain Edward English attempted to steer the ship toward a sandy cove, but the waves carried the ship over a sharp-ridged reef and eventually trapped the vessel among the rocks.

Historians credit Tang, the massive canine, for the rescue of the ninety-two sailors on board. With a rope in his mouth, he jumped into the icy waters and swam to shore, where he was met by people on the beach who secured the line and used it to rescue the sailors.[25]

Animals of Valor

The People's Dispensary for Sick Animals (PDSA) was founded in 1917 by Maria Dickin. Its mission was to provide care for sick and injured animals belonging to the poor in the United Kingdom. In 1943, the PDSA instituted the Dickin Medal, an award to honor the gallantry of animals during times of war. Here are some of their stories:

Judy, English Pointer
Prisoner No 81A, Gloergoer Camp at Medan,
Indonesia 1942–1945
Date of Award: May 1946
Judy, an English pointer and a member of the Royal Navy of the British Armed Forces, was aboard the HMS Grasshopper during World War II before it was marooned in Indonesia in 1942. The Japanese had conquered that country and captured the men,

along with Judy, where they were held as prisoners of war in Japan.

Judy was treated harshly by the brutal prison guards, but she survived their attacks, raised the morale of the British prisoners, and eventually struck up a close friendship with leading aircraftsman Frank Williams. Frank was able to smuggle Judy aboard a Japanese prisoner transport ship, which was hit by a torpedo on its way to Singapore in 1944. The ship sank, and Judy saved many men by pushing debris towards them to keep them afloat. She made it to shore, where she was reunited with Frank in another POW camp. They remained there together until the war's end in 1945.

Frank took Judy home with him to Britain, where she lived peacefully until she died from a tumor in 1950 at age thirteen.

G.I. Joe, Pigeon
No USA 43 SC 6390
Date of Award: August 1946

In October 1943, the United States had planned to bomb the village of Calvi Vecchia, twenty-five miles north of Naples, Italy. The Americans believed the village was a German stronghold, but little did they know that the Germans had abandoned the village and the British 169th Infantry had taken control of it.

As radio communications failed, the British sent American G. I. Joe, carrying a written message to a U.S. airbase, some twenty miles away across enemy territory. G. I. Joe arrived just as the bombers were warming up, saving up to one thousand lives.

Theo, Spaniel Cross
Royal Army Veterinary Corps Arms and Explosives Search Dog, Afghanistan
Date of Award: October 2012

Theo and his companion, Lance Corporal Liam Tasker, age twenty-six, were stationed together in Afghanistan. Their mission: bomb detection. Theo received the Dickin Award posthumously for breaking the record for most operational finds by an arms-and-explosives search dog. He suffered a seizure and died just hours after Tasker was killed by the Taliban in 2011.

Olga, Bay Mare
Metropolitan Police Service, London
Date of Award: April 1947

On July 3, 1944, Olga and her rider, J. E. Thwaites, were patrolling in south London, near the railway line, when a bomb exploded three hundred feet away. The explosion killed four people and destroyed homes, causing a plate-glass window to come crashing down right in front of Olga. Although she was startled and attempted to run from the scene, her rider was quickly able to calm her. The pair returned to the area and worked to control the crowd so that the wounded could be cared for.[26]

Apollo, German Shepherd
New York City K-9 Unit, Search and Rescue
Date of Award: March 2002

Apollo, a German shepherd search-and-rescue dog, was working for the New York Police Department in the K-9 unit on September 11, 2001, when the World Trade Center was attacked by terrorists.

The first search-and-rescue dog to arrive on the scene—just fifteen minutes after the attack—Apollo fell into a pool during his mission, drenching himself with water (the plunge was credited as saving his life, because soon afterwards, he was hit by falling debris and fire). His handler, Peter Davis, brushed him off, and Apollo went right back to work.

Apollo received the Dickin Medal for his tireless courage and service to humanity on behalf of all of the search-and-rescue canines on that mission. He died in November 2006.[27]

Simon, Cat
British Royal Navy, Rat Sniper
Date of Award: 1949

Simon was stationed on the Royal Navy HMS Amethyst during the Chinese Civil War in 1949. His duty was rat sniping, and he was especially good at it.

On April 20, 1949, the ship was traveling up the Yangtze River, from Shanghai to Nanking, when about halfway along their journey, they were fired on by the People's Liberation Army. During the attack, the captain was killed and the ship became grounded on the shore, its engines left inoperable. Simon was also injured in the attack, but was cared for by the crew and recovered from his injuries.

The crew remained trapped there for three months, during which time the ship was overrun by rats. But, as soon as Simon recovered from his injuries, he went back to his task of rat sniper, and did so with great energy, protecting the ship's food supply and raising the morale of the crew.

After they escaped from the river, Simon was awarded the Dickin Medal for disposal of many rats despite injury. He died while quarantined in the United Kingdom on November 28, 1949.[28]

Kaiser, German Shepherd
Army 24th Scout Dog Platoon
1965

Kaiser and his partner, Marine Lance Corporal Alfredo Salazar, were flown into Vietnam on December 3, 1965. During their tour, they completed more than thirty combat missions and led many soldiers to safety. Kaiser was the first dog to be killed in action in the Vietnam War. He was killed in 1966 during an enemy attack by the Viet Cong, but not before leading many soldiers on that same mission to safety. His platoon buried him at their unit campsite, which they then named Camp Kaiser.[29]

Sergeant Stubby, Boston Bull Terrier
102nd Infantry, 26th (Yankee) Division
1918

Sergeant Stubby, so named after his short tail, joined the 102 Infantry, 26th (Yankee) Division in the spring of 1918. Just a puppy at the time, he was smuggled aboard the S. S. Minnesota in Virginia later that summer, and set sail for France.

Having entered the war's front lines in February, 1918, over the next eighteen months, Stubby participated in seventeen World War I engagements, including four offensives. He has been credited with saving his regiment from gas attacks, finding and comforting the wounded, and even catching and holding a German spy until American soldiers arrived.

Because of his bravery in combat and success on the battle-field, he was promoted to Sergeant, and became the first and most decorated war dog of World War I. He became a celebrity back home in America, and even had the honor of meeting two United States presidents, Warren G. Harding and Calvin Coolidge.

Stubby died in the spring of 1926, and his remains are preserved at the Smithsonian Institute.[30]

chapter sixteen

When Heaven Intervenes

By Terry James

For those of us who love our furry family members, there is no question that the tugs at our hearts stem from some special, unseen source. As a matter of fact, the daily bonding we experience has—for us—an undeniable *spiritual* quality. We sense a supernatural tie in some cases, as I believe has been demonstrated in some of the stories of my own family pets and our interactions with them.

We believe that these special companions are God-given from the beginning, when Adam was privileged to name them. That there seems to be a special, heavenly presence around them at times is apparent. The thought that there is heavenly interaction with and through the animal world in general is validated by the actual news reports that follow.

Hero Parrot "Willie" Saves Choking Girl

DENVER—A parrot whose cries of alarm alerted his owner when a little girl choked on her breakfast has been honored as a hero.

Willie, a Quaker parrot, has been given the local Red Cross chapter's Animal Lifesaver Award....

Willie's owner, Megan Howard, was baby-sitting for a toddler. Howard left the room and the little girl, Hannah, started to choke on her breakfast.

Willie repeatedly yelled "Mama, baby" and flapped his wings, and Howard returned in time to find the girl already turning blue.

Howard saved Hannah by performing the Heimlich maneuver but said Willie "is the real hero."[31]

Hero Cat Roused Sleeping Owner as
Carbon Monoxide Filled Family's Home

NEW CASTLE, IND.—A cat helped spare a family from death by carbon monoxide poisoning by jumping on the bed and meowing wildly as fumes filled the home, the owners said.

Eric and Cathy Keesling said their 14-year-old cat, Winnie, played a crucial role in saving their lives March 24 after a gasoline-powered water pump in their basement caused the odorless but deadly gas to build up.

About 1 a.m., the domestic shorthair began nudging Cathy's ear and meowing loudly.

"It was a crazy meow, almost like she was screaming," said Cathy, who hesitated to get up until Winnie's caterwauling and jumping persisted.

When she finally climbed from bed, she realized she was nauseous and dizzy and couldn't awaken her husband. Because he had undergone minor neck surgery the previous day, she decided to call 911 but was so disoriented she had trouble dialing.

Paramedics found the couple's 14-year-old son, Michael, unconscious on the floor near his bedroom. The Keeslings were taken from the home in oxygen masks, treated for carbon monoxide poisoning and soon recovered.

Cathy Keesling said Winnie acted similarly last summer when tornadoes tore through the area, 45 miles east of Indianapolis.

"I really believe cats can sense these kind of things," she said.[32]

Rabbit Saves Diabetic from Coma

A diabetic man is crediting his giant pet rabbit with saving his life when he slipped into a coma.

Simon Steggall, 42, of Warboys in Cambridgeshire, said Dory, a one-and-a-half stone rabbit, jumped on his chest and thumped furiously when he passed out while watching television.

Dory's odd behaviour caught the attention of Mr. Steggall's wife, Victoria, 32, an ambulance driver.

When her attempts to bring him round failed, she rang 999 for paramedics for help.

"I work for the ambulance service and I'm embarrassed that the rabbit spotted it before I did," Mrs. Steggall said.

"When I told my specialist about what had happened he said he had heard of cats and dogs acting this way, but never a rabbit."

Mr. Steggall said his wife thought he had simply nodded off.

"When I have one of these turns I can't speak or move, but I can still hear and I heard Victoria tell Dory to get down.

"Although she is a house rabbit, she's not allowed on the furniture. The rabbit came up on my lap and started tapping and digging at my chest and looking at my face.

"That caught Victoria's attention and she realised something was wrong."

Mr. Steggall, a diabetic since childhood who has to inject insulin four times each day, said he did not get any warning when he was about to be unwell.

"One moment I am vertical and next minute I am waking up with a paramedic. It's like a flick of a switch."

The couple have had Dory, a three-foot rabbit, for three months, but she is not the first pet to respond when he has a diabetic reaction.

Mr. Steggall said he once had a black Labrador who would cower in a corner when his blood sugar levels began to fall dangerously low—reminding him do a blood test.[33]

Horse Rides to Rescue as Owner Attacked
in Field by Raging Cow
CAMBRIDGESHIRE, GREAT BRITAIN—A farmer has told how

she was saved by her horse after it fought off a raging cow that was attacking her.

Fiona Boyd, 40, feared she was going to be crushed to death by the half-ton cow after it kicked her to the ground, then rolled on top of her.

She had been about to guide the normally placid animal and its calf towards a shed when the cow suddenly attacked.

She believes she survived only because her horse, Kerry, raced to the rescue and kicked the cow until it moved off her.

Yesterday, Mrs Boyd said: "I am in no doubt Kerry saved me. If she hadn't been grazing in the same pasture, I really believe I would have been killed. Kerry was fantastic. She saved my life."

Despite her ordeal Mrs Boyd escaped serious injury."[34]

Family's "Angel" Dog Saves Boy from Cougar Attack

BOSTON BAR, BRITISH COLUMBIA—One lucky boy in Canada can say without a doubt that he has his own personal guardian angel—not of the spiritual kind, but of the furry.

On Saturday an 18-month old golden retriever saved her owner from being attacked by a cougar while in the backyard of their home in Boston Bar, British Columbia, about 130 miles north of Vancouver.

The dog—named Angel—leaped into action and threw herself between her owner, 11-year-old Austin Forman, and the cougar that was charging at him.

Sherri Forman, Austin's mother, said her son was outside with Angel around 5:30 p.m. gathering firewood from their backyard. She explained that Angel normally runs around and plays when she is outside, but on this afternoon she was behaving differently.

"He had come in at one point to tell me how cute Angel was being because she was sticking pretty close to him in the yard, which was unusual for her," Forman told CNN.

In hindsight she realizes that Angel was protecting her son from an unseen danger.

When the cougar charged, Angel ran to protect the boy.

"She intercepted the cougar," Forman said. "Austin came into the house very upset, and I had to get him to calm down so I could understand what he was saying. Finally he said 'there's a cougar eating Angel.'"

Angel and the cougar fought under the family's deck, while Austin's mother called 911 for help. A constable was in the area and able to make it to their home and kill the cougar quickly.

Forman said when her nephew pulled the cougar's body off Angel, who at first appeared fatally injured, the dog sucked in a "big breath of air and then got up." Ever the protector, Angel "walked to Austin, sniffed him to make sure he was alright, then sat down." Despite receiving a few deep bites and scratches Angel's prognosis is good."[35]

LuLu the Heroic Pig Now Known Worldwide
Her Fame and Girth Still Growing

PITTSBURGH—Once upon a time in a land not far away—Beaver Falls, to be exact—Jo Ann and Jack Altsman agreed to babysit their daughter's Vietnamese pot-bellied pig, LuLu.

LuLu endeared herself to the Altsmans, and they to her. Daughter Jackie kept putting off fetching her pet, and before long, LuLu belonged to Jack and Jo Ann.

LuLu grew and grew, from 4 pounds in 1997 to a whopping 150 a year later, but with each pound the attachment between the couple and the porker grew, too.

Happier a couple there had never been when, on Aug. 4, 1998, LuLu showed herself to be more than just a pig with a penchant for jelly donuts. Jo Ann says it was magical.

Jack was fishing on Lake Erie when Jo Ann, 61, had a heart attack, her second in 18 months.

She threw an alarm clock through a window of their vacation trailer at Presque Isle and yelled for help—all to no avail. Bear, their dog, an American Eskimo, just barked.

LuLu cried "big, fat tears," Jo Ann recalled, but she didn't cry all the way home. She knew what to do.

She squeezed through the doggy door and somehow pushed open the gate. According to villagers, she then lay down in traffic.

One nice man eventually stopped and followed LuLu to the trailer. Seeing the cuts LuLu had suffered on her stomach in squeezing through the small doggy door, the man yelled, "Lady, your pig's in distress."

"I'm in distress, too," came the reply. "Please call an ambulance."

Jo Ann was flown to The Medical Center, Beaver, for open-heart surgery. Had 15 more minutes passed, doctors told her, she would have died.[36]

Wildlife Heroes

Pets aren't the only members of the animal kingdom who deserve the heroes' crowns of our troubled, tumultuous world. The wildlife heroes continually perform what seem truly supernatural feats.

Dolphins Save Surfer from Becoming Shark's Bait

MONTEREY, CALIFORNIA—Surfer Todd Endris needed a miracle. The shark—a monster great white that came out of nowhere—had hit him three times, peeling the skin off his back and mauling his right leg to the bone.

That's when a pod of bottlenose dolphins intervened, forming a protective ring around Endris, allowing him to get to shore, where quick first aid provided by a friend saved his life.

"Truly a miracle," Endris told TODAY's Natalie Morales....

The attack occurred on Tuesday, Aug. 28, just before 11 a.m. at Marina State Park off Monterey, Calif., where the 24-year-old owner of Monterey Aquarium Services had gone with friends for a day of the sport they love....

The shark, estimated at 12 to 15 feet long, hit him first as Endris was sitting on his surfboard, but couldn't get its monster jaws around both surfer and surfboard. "The second time, he came down and clamped on my torso — sandwiched my board and my torso in his mouth," Endris said....

The third time, the shark tried to swallow Endris' right leg, and he said that was actually a good thing, because the shark's grip anchored him while he kicked the beast in the head and snout with his left leg until it let go.

The dolphins, which had been cavorting in the surf all along, showed up then. They circled him, keeping the shark at bay, and enabled Endris to get back on his board and catch a wave to the shore.[37]

Whale Saves Drowning Diver, Pulls Her to Surface

HARBIN, CHINA—A beluga whale saved a drowning diver by hoisting her to the surface, carrying her leg in its mouth.

Terrified Yang Yun thought she was going to die when her legs were paralyzed by crippling cramps in arctic temperatures. Competitors had to sink to the bottom of an aquarium's 20-foot arctic pool and stay there for as long as possible with the beluga whales at Polar Land in Harbin, north east China.

But when Yun, 26, tried to head to the surface she struggled to move her legs.

"I began to choke and sank even lower and I thought that was it for me—I was dead. Until I felt this incredible force under me driving me to the surface," Yun said.

Beluga whale Mila had spotted her difficulties and using her sensitive dolphin-like nose guided Yun safely to the surface.[38]

Gorilla at an Illinois Zoo Rescues a 3-Year-Old Boy

CHICAGO—A 3-year-old boy fell into an exhibit occupied by gorillas at the Brookfield Zoo [near Chicago] this afternoon, and was rescued by a female gorilla that cradled the child and brought him to zookeepers.

The boy injured his head when he fell 18 feet onto the exhibit's concrete. He was alert when taken to a hospital, although his condition was later listed as critical.

Seven gorillas were on display in the exhibit. One of them, Binti, a 7-year-old female with a baby gorilla on her back, picked up the child, cradled him in her arms and placed him near a door where zookeepers could retrieve him, said Sondra Katzen, a spokeswoman for the zoo.[39]

Lions Save African Girl from Abductors

ADDIS ABABA, ETHIOPIA—A 12-year-old girl who was abducted and beaten by men trying to force her into a marriage was found being guarded by three lions who apparently had chased off her captors, a policeman said Tuesday.

The girl, missing for a week...was beaten repeatedly before she was found June 9 by police and relatives on the outskirts of Bita Genet.... She had been guarded by the lions for about half a day.[40]

chapter seventeen

The Amazing Pet Industry

By Dana Neel

Gas prices are keeping travelers closer to home these days, and the cost of groceries has turned many shoppers into conscientious coupon clippers. The shaky economy has conditioned most of us in America to keep a close eye on the bank balance and a tight grip on our money.

But when it comes to our pets, we apparently aren't cutting any corners. In fact, there seem to be no limits to the cash we're willing to plunk down to protect and pamper our pets—from birth to burial. —And that's despite rising unemployment rates, falling stock prices, and ongoing uncertainty about the future because of the never-ending turbulence in our nation's capital.

In fact, even during the recession years between 2008–2010, America's retail pet spending didn't slow down; it increased by 11.9 percent. And in 2011, American families spent more on feeding and caring for their pets—a whopping $61.4 billion—than they did on movies, video games, and music combined. The pet industry is the seventh-largest retail industry in the United States, with sales that exceed those of the hardware, jewelry, toy, and candy businesses.[41] But, that's not a hard statistic to get your brain around, when you consider that nearly 75 percent of American households own some 218 million pets (not including fish)!

Pets don't just have hold of our heart strings (as the stories in this book have abundantly illustrated); they seem to have control of our purse strings as well. That's why we thought it might be fun to have a look at a few of the ways we're spending our money on our pets, and at some of the trends in the surprisingly posh pet arena of products.

Feeding Fido and Fluffy

Gone are the days of throwing a ten-pound bag of dry kibble onto the lower rack of the shopping buggy at Wal-Mart, figuring that will be enough to keep the family dog fed and happy for the next couple of weeks.

Instead, we've gone gourmet, gluten-free, and green.

"If there's a trend in human food and supplements, you'll see it on the pet food aisle," according to Bob Vetere, president of the Greenwich, Connecticut-based American Pet Products Association (APPA). "Gluten-free, vitamin supplemented, breed-specific, senior formulas—all of these have taken over the pet marketplace, and we're seeing the competition increasing."[42]

Pet owners in the United States spent nearly $20 billion on pet food alone in 2011 and are projected to spend more than $26 billion annually by 2015,[43] with much of the market's growth in organic, natural, and premium foods. The market for these types of foods accounts for nearly 32 percent of the entire pet food market.[44]

Although natural pet foods can be considerably more expensive than commercially prepared food, pet owners can be quite passionate about their decision to care for their pets, just as they would any other family member, including providing a specialty diet that they view as more wholesome.[45]

At a number of the big-box pet stores such as Petco and Petsmart, as well as a variety of the smaller pet boutiques, you can find all kinds of gourmet foods, including minimally processed raw foods and those that boast certain ingredients such as glucosamine, chondroitin, green lipped mussel, and sea cucumber.[46]

Other pet-food producers market their brands for the humane way in which the food was obtained, such as free-range; and also for what the food lacks rather than what it contains, as in gluten-free, corn-free, byproduct-free, hormone-free, antibiotic-free, and so on. And if you don't think your pet's diet is well balanced enough, even after giving him or her these specialized foods, you can also find a variety of supplements, including omega-3, alfalfa, blueberries, garlic, and brewer's yeast to provide your pet with clear eyes, a shiny coat, and healthy joints.[47]

The Care and Keeping of those Beloved, Fur-coated Creatures

Pampering our pets doesn't stop at a nutrient-supplemented, gourmet diet. Two of the fastest-growing areas in the pet industry are specialty grooming, including spa treatments and massage, and pet daycare and boarding services.

According to the APPA, the pet sector that showed the highest growth in 2012 was pet services (grooming, boarding, daycare, pet sitting etc.), with an increase of 9.1 percent from 2011 to 2012, for a total of $4.16 billion in spending.

"Increased high-end grooming services are fueling new growth in the high income end of the category along with increased use of all services," said APPA President and CEO Bob Vetere.[48]

Consider the Chateau Poochie in Pompano Beach, Florida, an exceptionally grand hotel for canines and felines. This hotel offers a variety of suites with amenities such as chef-prepared gourmet meals, five daily walks, classical music, filtered water, fleece bedding, flat screen TVs, air conditioning, and tuck-in services.

For your favorite feline, the Palace Cat Boudoir is a three-tiered, deluxe condo filled with an entertaining virtual coral reef, private powder room, and engaging window views. The hotel's minibar service includes items such as holistic biscuits, bone cakes, dental treats, and pig ears.[49]

Upon check-in at the Chateau, your beloved pet will be offered a variety of al a carte services, including an aromatherapy bath, full-body massage, warm-wax treatment, hair coloring, facial, a "pawdicure" complete with nail polish, and even an extreme makeover. Additionally, four-legged friends can participate in fitness and training classes, and even socialize with other guests at the hotel's Doggie Disco & Social Lounge.[50]

The Chateau Poochie isn't the only pet hotel where pets can get the all-star treatment. The Pet Hotel at Barkingham Palace in Palm Desert, California, bills itself as a luxury hotel for pet boarding, daycare, and recreation. Having a variety of elegantly appointed suites to choose from, they also have onsite staff twenty-four hours each day, and webcam service so you can watch your pet enjoying his or her experiences while there.

Whether you need to drop off your pet for an afternoon while you play a round of golf, or for an extended stay while you are away on vacation, The Barkingham facility also provides luxuries such as specialty spa services, including warm-water pool therapy, hydrating masks, and full-body massage. And, to keep fit, pets can participate in Pilates classes and treadmill runs. For social and recreational opportunities, the grounds feature several off-leash parks with playground equipment, swimming pools, and other water features.

Do you have a pet wedding or birthday coming up? The Hotel at Barkingham Palace will be happy to accommodate your pet and guests for these celebrations.[51]

Gift-Giving for Pets

For that special wedding or birthday party, online sites and pet boutiques offer no shortage of pet gifts. A recent search at "Google" for "gifts for pets" returned 136 million hits! Results featured products ranging from treats and toys—such as a dog biscuit maker for your kitchen and an interactive laser light to entertain your cat—to more practical items, such as furniture, bedding, and clothing.

Nine out of ten pet owners consider their pets as members of the family, so of course they will be acknowledged during holidays! According to a recent PetFinder.com poll, Americans spend about $5 billion annually on holiday presents for their pets. At Christmastime, 63 percent of dog owners and 58 percent of cat owners say they include pets in the gift-giving tradition, and 40 percent of dog owners and 37 percent of cat owners say they hang a Christmas stocking for their pets.[52]

We not only buy our pets gifts for the holidays, but we also include them in the festivities, buying special clothing and costumes as part of our celebrations. Whether its reindeer antlers or Santa hats at Christmastime or a wide variety of costumes for Halloween, our pets are very much a part of our families and are treated as such. According to the National Retail Federation, of the 70 percent of American families who planned to celebrate Halloween in 2012, more than 15 percent intended to include costumes for their pets. Spending on Halloween costumes for pets was projected to be $370 million dollars in 2012—a full

$70 million dollars more than what families spent dressing up their canines, felines, and other beloved creatures in 2011.[53]

When Our Pets Die

When the festivities have faded and the years have passed, sadly, there comes a time when we must part ways with our furry friends and celebrate their lives as they go home to be with our Lord. Thankfully, there are many options to help us as we prepare our pets for their journey to Heaven.

According to the International Association of Pet Cemeteries and Crematories in Atlanta, Georgia, just a decade ago, there were very few facilities in the country that provided services to honor family pets at the end of life. Today, there are nearly seven hundred pet funeral homes, cemeteries, and crematories in the United States. Although there are no statistical data on profitability, families spent more than $52 billion on these services in 2011.

Bob Walczyk from Green Bay, Wisconsin, is the owner of Forever Friends, a funeral home and crematory for pets. He is also the owner of the funeral business next door, which is exclusively for humans. In an interview with a *Bloomberg Business Week* writer for an article entitled, "There's Never Been a Better Time to Be a Dead Pet," Walczyk described a common scenario: "When people come to the funeral home and I tell them how much it is to cremate their grandfather, it's never cheap enough for them," says Walczyk. "They'll say, 'How much? You've got to be kidding me!'

"But when the exact same family brings their dog next door, they don't even ask about money. They just tell me what they want and they take out their checkbook."[54]

It used to be common to leave the aftercare of our pets up to the veterinarian, but times have changed. In 2003, Coleen Ellis opened the nation's first pet funeral home, the Pet Angel Memorial Center in Indianapolis, Indiana. After the death of her beloved terrier-schnauzer Mico, she made it her mission to change the way animals were treated after death, and to help families navigate the options of aftercare. She fully understood from personal experience that this is a time of deep grief and the options were few.[55]

Ellis founded the Pet Loss Professionals Alliance, a group developed to give more formality and ethics to the pet loss industry. She advocated for individual cremation and worked to see that every veterinary clinic in the country provided information on the care of aging animals, including planning for aftercare. But mostly, she fought to change the stigma against pet owners who wish to have formal ceremonies for their pets, including caskets, flowers, and funeral services. These people were previously labeled as eccentrics or loners, simply for viewing their pets as family members. But, thanks to the work of Ellis and others, this stereotype is rapidly fading as the pet aftercare industry has become established in America.[56]

Forever Friends

In His Sermon on the Mount, Jesus said that where we spend our money is an indication of the loyalties of our heart (see Matthew 6:19–21). We've seen abundant proof of that in this chapter! We pet lovers are a loyal breed, to be sure, willing to spend much of our personal resources—not to mention our time and energy—on pampering our much-loved furry friends. (It's true that the extravagant figures statistics show us might seem hard to comprehend or justify, considering the financial hardships suffered by many in our country and around the world. We simply report these amazing facts—we're not recommending or lauding lavish financial outlay. We hope that each individual who is spending these kinds of dollars on his or her pets is relying on the biblical principles of good stewardship to guide spending in every category of life—including the one that's the focus of this book.)

Of course, Jesus intended His words to serve as a warning against counting on our earthly treasures—like bank accounts, baseball cards, and speedboats—as being of any potential eternal value. However, pet lovers like those of us who have been involved in the publication of this book, and like those of you who are reading it, will find great hope and comfort in the realization that our pets are not "things" to be merely counted among the inventory of "earthly treasures" we accumulate. As has been clearly explained in previous chapters, God uses pets (and in fact all animals) in a number of ways to bring about His eternal purposes during life as we know it on earth. He can use them to shape our character, to show us compassion, and to provide us with companionship. He can use them to provide us with joy, to teach us responsibility, and to demonstrate unconditional love. He can even use them to physically save someone's life!

So, considering all that's wrapped up in our surprisingly complex and obviously God-ordained relationships with our pets, it's a blessing beyond measure to know that they will continue to be part of His eternal plan for us even after they (and we) die—treasures in Heaven, indeed!

Conclusion
(But Not the End!)

By Terry James

To repeat earlier thoughts expressed in these pages, man's involvement with the animal—man's love for the animal world—is the tie that seems to link the Creator with His two distinct created beings, man and animal. And to repeat further, it is absolutely imperative that we believe God when He says that He gave us—mankind—dominion over the animal kingdom. It is essential to understand and believe that God meant what He said when He saw fit to inform us that He created us, made us, in His own image. Because that truth came from the Creator's own mind, we can be sure that He intended our ultimate destiny, our life after death, to include eternal powers not unlike His own. To have dominion over a thing is to have power over it.

Remember that the Almighty Creator told us in the book of Ecclesiastes that both man and animal have physical bodies that die and return to the dust. The spirit of man at death goes upward, that is, it never stays with the body that returns to dust. Man's spirit returns to God because He, the Creator, has dominion, or power, over His creation, man. The spirit of the beast (or animal) goes into the ground to be with the body that returns to dust. But take heart! The important thing to know is that just as man has a spirit, so the animal has a spirit. The spirit of the animal is obviously different from the soul of man, but the animal, God's Word says, has a spirit.

God also says, in many instances, that He calls the souls of those whom He loves and who also love Him to return to Him upon physical death. The spirit He gave, He has the power and the right to receive unto Himself again.

God has said in very specific terms that He made man in His own image. He then made the animals, but determined in His omniscience to give man dominion, that is power, over the beasts of the earth, each of whom has a spirit. God, in His all-knowing will, for His own good purposes, gave man God-likeness, which will reach its full potential only when God and man reunite for eternity.

Is there life after death for the pets we love? When we look into the sweet faces of those furry little family members, their wide eyes so trusting, so happy to take in all the love we can give them, can there be any doubt that the love is a mutual thing? Can there be any question that those delightful moments of the loving, understanding, come from a thing much more profound than mere physical attraction?

The Creator's word tells us: "But as it is written, Eye hath not seen, nor ear heard, neither have entered into the heart of man, the things which God hath prepared for them that love him" (1 Corinthians 2:9). One of those marvelous things is that when we have attained our ultimate God-likeness, we will be able to recall the spirits of those pets we love so much from the dust of the earth just as the Creator recalls the spirits of those who love Him into his own majestic presence at the moment of physical life's cessation.

Is there life after death for the pets we love? I'm counting on it!

Notes

1. Corry Kanzenberg, Curator of Archival Collections, Norman Rockwell Museum, "Rockwell's Dogs," http://thebark.com/content/rockwells-dogs.

2. Randy Alcorn, *Eternal Perspectives: A Collection of Quotations on Heaven, the New Earth, and Life after Death* (Tyndale House Publishers: 2012), 437.

3. Joni Eareckson Tada, *Holiness in Hidden Places* (Nashville: J. Countryman, 1999), 133.

4. Randy Alcorn, "Will There Be Animals in Heaven?" *Eternal Perspective Ministries*, February 3, 2010: http://www.epm.org/resources/2010/Feb/3/will-there-be-animals-heaven/.

5. Peter Kreeft, *Every Thing You Ever Wanted to Know about Heaven but Never Dreamed of Asking* (Ignatius Press, SF: 1990), 45.

6. W. A. Criswell and Page Patterson, *Heaven* (Wheaton: Tyndale House Publishers, 1991), 53.

7. Alcorn, *Eternal Perspectives,* 388.

8. C. S. Lewis, *The Great Divorce* (New York: Simon & Schuster, 1996), 106–107.

9. C. S. Lewis, *The Problem of Pain* (ed. 3, reprint: Macmillan, 1962), 124–126.

10. "Most Popular Pet Names," http://www.petbabynames.com/.

11. Julie Morris, "Breed Rescue," Petfinder.com.

12. "Famous Bulldog Gallery," http://www.cesarsway.com/newsandevents/celebritydogs/Gallery-of-Famous-Bulldogs-1.

13. "Everyday Care of Your Bulldog," http://www.bulldoginformation.com/everyday-care-of-your-bulldog.html.

14. "Felix the Cat: History," http://www.felixthecat.com/history.html.

15. Wikipedia contributors, "Morris the Cat," *Wikipedia, The Free Encyclopedia,* http://en.wikipedia.org/w/index.php?title=Morris_the_Cat&oldid=558982672.

16. Paul Ciempanelli, "Seeing Eye to Eye—Comparing Cat and Dog Vision," Paw Nation, July 28, 2011, http://www.pawnation.com/2011/07/28/seeing-eye-to-eye-comparing-cat-and-dog-vision/3.

17. Hayley Hudson, "Blind Dog and Guide Cat Go on Walks Together," http://www.huffingtonpost.com/2013/01/01/blind-dogs-guide-cat-take_n_2388956.html.

18. Jeanie Lerche Davis, "Five Ways Pets Can Improve Your Health," http://www.webmd.com/hypertension-high-blood-pressure/features/5-ways-pets-improve-your-health.

19. "Interesting Facts About Dogs," MSPCA/Angell, http://www.mspca.org/programs/pet-owner-resources/pet-owner-guides/dog-care-adoption/interesting-facts-dogs.html.

20. "Dog Facts," Animal Planet, http://animal.discovery.com/pets/dog-facts.htm.

21. "Home Remedies: Pets," *The Old Farmer's Almanac,* http:/www.almanac.com/content/home-remedies-pets.

22. "It's Snoopy Trivia Time, Charlie Brown," http://www.pet360.com/dog/breeds/its-snoopy-trivia-time-charlie-brown/vcZmAAioZU2pbE2XNlsECw.

23. "Biography for Rin Tin Tin," IMDb (Internet Movie Database), http://www.imdb.com/name/nm0863833/bio?ref=nm_ov_bio_sm.

24. Andrea Thompson, "What's the Most Popular Pet?" Live Science, http://www.livescience.com/32415-whats-the-most-popular-pet. html.

25. "10 Remarkable Animals that Have Saved Lives," Mother Nature Network, http://www.mnn.com/earth-matters/animals/photos/10-remarkable-animals-that-have-saved-lives/92-stranded-sailors-saved; Mary Bridson, "Hero, the Phantom Dog, History, Myth, and Journalism," http://www.newfoundlandshipwrecks.com/Ethie/Documents/hero_the_phantom_dog.htm; Maryann Mott, "Guard Dogs: Newfoundlands' Lifesaving Past, Present, National Geographic News, February 7, 2003, http://news.nationalgeographic.com/news/2003/02/0207_030207_newfies.html.

26. Information derived for these sections is compiled from the following entries in Wikipedia, the Free Encyclopedia, "The Dickin Medal," http://en.wikipedia.org/wiki/Dickin_Medal; "Judy (dog)," http://en.wikipedia.org/wiki/Judy_(dog); "G. I. Joe (pigeon)," http://en.wikipedia.org/wiki/G.I._Joe_(pigeon); "Theo (dog)," http://en.wikipedia.org/wiki/Theo_(dog); and "Equine Recipients of the Dickin Medal," http://en.wikipedia.org/wiki/Olga_(horse)#Olga; as well as from the following news source: Julian Gavaghan, "Animal Heroes: The Cat Who Killed 'Mao Tse Tung,' the Pigeon Who Saved 1,00 Lives, and Other Incredible Stories," Yahoo News, March 13, 2013, http://news.yahoo.com/animal-heroes--the-cat-who-killed--mao-tse-tung---the-pigeon-who-saved-1-000-lives-and-other-incredible-stories-183304918.html.

27. Wikipedia, the Free Encyclopedia, "Apollo (dog)," http://en.wikipedia.org/wiki/Appollo_(dog).

28. Wikipedia, the Free Encyclopedia, "Dickin Medal," http://en.wikipedia.org/wiki/Dickin_Medal; "Simon (cat)," http://en.wikipedia.org/wiki/Simon_(cat); and "HMS *Amethyst* (F116)," http://en.wikipedia.org/wiki/HMS_Amethyst_(F116).

29. Avery Mann, "Famous Military Working Dogs," *American Profile,* November 23, 2011, http://americanprofile.com/articles/famous-military-working-dogs/.
30. Wikipedia, the Free Encyclopedia, "Sergeant Stubby," http://en.wikipedia.org/wiki/Sergeant_Stubby; "Military Working Dog Teams National Monument," World War I—Sergeant Stubby, http://www.jbmf.us/hst-ww1.aspx.
31. *The Huffington Post,* "Hero Parrot Willie Saves Choking Girl," March 24, 2009, http://www.huffingtonpost.com/2009/03/24/hero-parrot-willie-saves-_n_178586.html.
32. Associated Press, "Hero Cat Roused Sleeping Owner as Carbon Monoxide Filled Family Home," Fox News, April 5, 2007, http://www.foxnews.com/story/2007/04/05/hero-cat-roused-sleeping-owner-as-carbon-monoxide-filled-family-home/.
33. BBC News, "Rabbit Saves Diabetic from Coma," January 29, 2004, http://news.bbc.co.uk/2/hi/uk_news/england/cambridgeshire/3441337.stm.
34. *The Scottsman*, "Horse Rides to Rescue as Owner Attacked in Field by Raging Cow," August 13, 2007, http://www.scotsman.com/news/scotland/top-stories/horse-rides-to-rescue-as-owner-attacked-in-field-by-raging-cow-1-913741.
35. Cheryl Robinson, "Family's 'Angel' Dog Saves Boy from Cougar Attack," CNN.com, January 5, 2010, http://www.cnn.com/2010/WORLD/americas/01/04/boy.cougar.attack/index.html.
36. Michael A. Fuoco, "LuLu the Heroic Pig Now Known Worldwide," *Post-Gazette,* April 9, 2002, http://old.post-gazette.com/neigh_west/20020409lulu0409p1.asp.
37. Mike Celizic, "Dolphins Save Surfer Becoming Shark's Bait," NBC News, *Today,* November 8, 2007, http://www.today.com/id/21689083/ns/today-today_people/t/dolphins-save-surfer-becoming-sharks-bait/#.UkitzYZ6YxN.

38. *The Sun,* "Whale Saves Drowning Diver, Pulls Her to Surface, Fox News, July 29, 2009, http://www.foxnews.com/story/2009/07/29/whale-saves-drowning-diver-pulls-her-to-surface/.

39. "Gorilla at an Illinois Zoo Rescues a 3-Year-Old Boy," *New York Times,* August 17, 1996, http://www.nytimes.com/1996/08/17/us/gorilla-at-an-illinois-zoo-rescues-a-3-year-old-boy.html.

40. Associated Press, "Lions Save African Girl from Abductors," Fox News, June 21, 2005, http://www.foxnews.com/story/2005/06/21/lions-save-african-girl-from-abductors/.

41. Steve Henderson, "Spending on Pets: 'Tails' from the Consumer Expenditure Survey," United States Department of Labor: Bureau of Labor Statistics, *Beyond the Numbers,* May 2013, Vol. 2, No. 16, http://www.bls.gov/opub/btn/volume-2/spending-on-pets.htm.

42. Jeannine Stein, "Pets Join in on the Organic Food Trend," *Los Angeles Times,* July 18, 2011, http://articles.latimes.com/2011/jul/18/health/la-he-pet-food-20110718.

43. According to the Pet Food Market Assessment of 2013, by the Packaging Machinery Manufacturers Institutes (PMMI).

44. "Petfood Market Driven by Growth in Specialty Pet Foods, PMMI Finds," *Food Market Assessment 2013,* PetFoodIndustry.com, February 11, 2013, http://www.petfoodindustry.com/47862.html.

45. Stein.

46. Petsmart, http://www.petsmart.com/product/index.jsp?productId=2750073&f=PAD%2FpsNotAvailInUS%2FNo.

47. Stein.

48. Alissa Wolf, "U.S. Pet Spending and Pet Ownership Statistics for 2012: APPA Reports Steady Growth," About.com, March 13, 2013, http://petshops.about.com/od/The-Paw-Sweet-Journal/a/US-Pet-Spending-And-Pet-Ownership-Statistics-For-2012.htm.

49. Chateau Poochie—It's a Dog's World, http://www.chateaupoochie.com/index.htm.

50. Ibid.
51. The Pet Hotel at Barkingham Palace, http://www.thepethotelatbarkinghampalace.com/.
52. American Humane Society, "FACTS—Pet Ownership," Petfinder.com, http://www.petfinder.com/for-shelters/facts-pet-ownership.html.
53. Kathy Grannis, "There's No Spooking Spending as Seven in 10 Americans Plan to Celebrate Halloween This Year," National Retail Federation, September 25, 2012, http://www.nrf.com/modules.php?name=News&op=viewlive&sp_id=1430.
54. Eric Spitznagel, "There's Never Been a Better Time to Be a Dead Pet," Bloomberg Business Week/Lifestyle, September 7, 2012, http://www.businessweek.com/articles/2012-09-07/theres-never-been-a-better-time-to-be-a-dead-pet.
55. Jessica Pierce, "All Dogs Go to Heaven: What Happens at a Pet Funeral Home?" *Psychology Today,* September 3, 2011, http://www.psychologytoday.com/blog/all-dogs-go-heaven/201112/what-happens-pet-funeral-home.
56. Ibid.